Exploring the Other Island

To Georgia,
for Travis,
and to others, including brothers Glenn and Craig
and several good friends, who despite being
"grown-up" continue to view the world
through the eyes of a child.

Exploring the Other Island

A Seasonal Guide to Nature

on

LONG ISLAND

John L. Turner

Photographs by

Robert T. McGrath and Marc Oliveri

WATERLINE BOOKS
GREAT FALLS, VIRGINIA
1994

This is a **Waterline** Natural History Book

WATERLINE BOOKS
438 River Bend Road
Great Falls, VA 22066
(703) 759-0368

ISBN: 0-9628492-2-7

Design and Composition: Greta D. Sibley
Front Cover: Long Island Pine Barrens (Robert T. McGrath)
Frontis: Saw-whet owl. (Robert T. McGrath)

First Printing, 1994

Contents

SUMMER

AUTUMN

Acknowledgments

Many books are collaborative efforts and such is the case with this one. I would like then to thank the following people, all accomplished naturalists, whose knowledge and insight significantly improved the book: Skip Blanchard, John Cryan, Andrew Greller, Eric Lamont, Robert McGrath, Drew Panko, Eric Salzman, Norman Soule and Craig Turner. I also thank Kay Liss for acting as matchmaker between the author and publisher. Special thanks to Bob McGrath and Marc Oliveri for providing photographs and to Maria Weisenberg for her seasonal illustrations.

Introduction

Writing in 1670, Daniel Denton captured the essence of primal Long Island when he canonized the wildflowers which caused "the countrey itself to send forth such a fragrant smell, that it may be perceived at Sea before they can make the Land." While it may be impossible to determine if it was Mr. Denton's nose or imagination that was his most sensitive feature, his perfumed image conjures up a picture of what the Island must have been like.

We know, for example, that gray wolves, bobcats and black bear once prowled the Island. Beaver were plentiful, and most of Long Island's streams had populations of "sea-run" brook trout. Alewife runs were numerous, and the timber rattlesnake once hunted the Island's underbrush. From the Oak Brush Plains and Pine Barrens came the booming mating call of the heath hen, the eastern race of the greater prairie chicken. Mountain lions, moose, elk and bison may also have roamed Long Island's forests, although the record of their presence is less certain.

The natural communities on Long Island were as diverse as the plant and animal species were abundant. The Hempstead Plains, a grassland composed of some of the same prairie grasses that make up the prairies of the midwest, stretched for some 60,000 acres (nearly 100 square miles) across central Nassau County. This striking area, the cause of which has never been satisfactorily explained, gave rise to the names of the modern-day communities of Plainedge and Plainview. Moving east, the prairie grasses intermingled with the islands of pitch pine and scrub oak of the Oak Brush Plains. The community of Island Trees owes its name to this unique transition zone. The Pine Barrens, encompassing the middle part of the Island, totaled nearly a quarter of a million acres.

In the western part of the Island, and along the north shore, virgin stands of oak, chestnut, hickory, beech and walnut formed a dense, shadowy forest rivaling those of the southern Appalachians. In moist soils the tulip tree, with its remarkable orange flowers, reached heights of 175 to 200 feet. Denton had something to say about the Island's forests as well as its flowers: "The greatest part of the Island is very full of timber, as oaks white and red, walnut trees, chestnut trees which yield store of mast for swine, also red maples, cedars, sarsifrage [sassafras?], Beach, Holly, Hazel with many more."

Another indication of the original richness and abundance of Long Island's flora lies in the text of an advertisement that ran in a late 1800s botanical journal. The ad features a list of 114 native shrubs and wildflowers for sale by a Mr. Elihu S. Miller of Wading River. (Mr. Miller helped develop the first list of native plants of Suffolk County.) Included are a number of insectivorous plants such as pitcher plants, half a dozen orchid species including pink lady slipper, ladies' tresses and rattlesnake plantain, and several fern species. Prices ran from $2.00 to $8.00. The amazing information lies in the heading of the ad. It reads: "LIST OF WILD PLANTS OF LONG ISLAND Which I am prepared to collect. The prices quoted are per hundred. I will deliver them at the Railroad packed in good order. Prices for single plants or per dozen by mail (postpaid) sent upon application."

Here was just one individual (and there must have been others) who made money presumably on a regular basis by picking wild plants in guaranteed quantities of 100. In contrast, if someone were to attempt to be so employed today (assuming it were legal to pick these species, and in most cases it is not), they would be out of business within a week. For some of the plant species Mr. Miller listed, there are not more than a few hundred plants remaining on all of Long Island.

The Long Island of today is not only diminished with regard to its wildflowers. The bobcat, wolf and bear are gone, having been exterminated early in the Island's settlement. The beaver, exploited beyond recovery, followed. The last heath hen perished in 1842 (and the last of its race died in 1931 on Martha's Vineyard), and the Labrador duck faded into extinction when the last known living specimen was shot on Long Island in 1875. The last rattlesnake was seen in 1912. A number of other species have vanished or have had their ranges substantially reduced.

Natural communities have suffered too. Virtually all of the Hempstead Plains, except for a token preserve, was destroyed due to the indifference of Nassau County officials. About 95 percent of the Oak Brush Plains has been lost, and more than half of the Pine Barrens as well. The great mixed deciduous forests on which Denton lavished praise were significantly cut over to supply lumber and cordwood, and after rebounding when the saws were stopped, became fragmented by suburban expansion. Thousands of acres of salt meadows which formed the southern edge of the Island have been buried beneath millions of tons of fill, placed there for tract housing.

Despite these profound changes, and the fact that nearly six million people now live here, there is still much that remains of the natural Island. Approximately 180 bird species have been recorded as breeding on Long Island and many more migrate through or overwinter here. Several dozen native mammals are found on Long Island and in the salty waters that surround it. Thousands of insect species feed upon the foliage of the Island's 88 or so native tree species or on the thousands of native shrubs, wildflowers and grasses.

It is my fond hope that the book will pique your interest in this "other" Long Island, the one that has always been there and is still available to those who care. Many fascinating natural events, unfolding seasonally, occur in full view at easy-to-get-to places. The book includes an assortment of the most interesting of these, accompanied by a list of specific places where the best examples can be enjoyed. This is my invitation to explore wildness, and by so doing, to become more deeply connected to the living world around you — an experience that is among the most fulfilling a human being can have.

A note of caution must be included concerning the welfare of plants and animals discussed in the book. Most wild animals are easily disturbed. Therefore, it is vital that a sufficient distance — common sense and the behavior of the animal are two good benchmarks — be maintained between the animal and its audience. Many of these animals are endangered and are afforded protection under various federal and state wildlife laws which contain stiff penalties for those who violate their provisions.

Appropriate judgment must be exercised with regard to plants as well. Many of the species detailed are rare and/or declining, and it is essential for their welfare that they not be dug up or picked. With the notable exception of blueberries and cranberries, leave the plant or wildflower there for the next person (or next generation) to enjoy.

SKUNK CABBAGE AND
SPRING PEEPERS.
(Maria T. Weisenberg)

Spring

YELLOW TROUT LILY. (Robert T. McGrath)

CHAPTER ONE

Spring Wildflowers

"WARM-BLOODED" AND SHORT-LIVED PLANTS

Selecting the quintessential sign of spring is certainly a subjective exercise. If you were to ask a group of naturalists to choose, however, perhaps a majority would pick the emergence of **skunk cabbage** in February. That skunk cabbage should rate so high is due both to its very early emergence and to the symbolism of the green and maroon streaked hoods as they break through the ice covering the wooded swamps where they grow: the botanical embodiment of spring conquering winter. Skunk cabbage is the first plant to bloom in a procession of flowers that runs through spring and summer on to the end of the blooming season in November. It has a secret weapon for getting a head start: it is "warm-blooded." More accurately, it is able to generate its own heat, an ability quite apparent by the melted ice or snow surrounding each hood.

Botanists who have studied this fascinating plant have found that as long as the air temperature remains above freezing, the temperature of the flower cluster, known botanically as a spadix, stays a balmy 72° F. Once the temperature drops below freezing, however, the spadix loses its heat-making ability and dies.

The plant generates heat the same way as animals do — by the consumption of oxygen in a process known as respiration. The fuel which energizes this activity is provided by starch that is stored in the large rootstock, which can be as much as two inches wide and a foot long in older plants. In addition to its heat-making ability, the skunk cabbage is remarkable in another way: measurements indicate that the temperature of the spadix is constant despite fluctuations in the air temperature. This means the plant is able to generate more or less heat as needed, suggesting that it has a built-in, yet undescribed thermostat. As one naturalist has said, "Skunk cabbage behaves more like a skunk than it does a cabbage!"

The hood of the skunk cabbage, technically known as the spathe, assists in keeping the plant warm. Its tissue is a spongy, biological styrofoam of sorts, made up of many tiny air spaces.

Why the skunk cabbage evolved the ability to generate heat is unclear. Blooming as early as it does, it seems logical to assume that higher temperatures help keep pollinating insects warm enough, and therefore active enough, to perform their vital chores. Also, the warmth seems to encourage the rapid growth of seeds which, dispersed early, have a greater chance to find a suitable location in which to germinate.

The conspicuous leaves of the plant emerge after the flower. Before long, the bunches of leaves, similar to tobacco in appearance, are all that is seen. Growing in colonies of hundreds or thousands in the mucky organic mat of the swamp, the knee-high plants lend a lush, primordial aspect to a wetland when fully leafed out.

In the moist woods, adjacent to the swampy wetlands where skunk cabbage dominates, grow a host of other wildflowers that bloom in early spring, about a month after the skunk cabbage. These are the **spring ephemerals.** The fragile looking flowers are so named because they bloom in early spring, persist awhile, and then die back. By early to midsummer they have disappeared, and a walk through their habitat at this time of year will reveal no sign of their existence.

Spring ephemerals may be employing the same tactic used by skunk cabbage. By blooming early, they have insect pollinators to themselves, thereby improving their chances for successful reproduction. Moreover, before the trees overhead can leaf out, the plants can capitalize on the unimpeded sunlight for photosynthetic food-making.

Wood anemone, also known as windflower, is a member of the buttercup family and has pretty, white, five-sepaled flowers. Like the flowering dogwood and marsh marigold, it lacks petals, and the sepals, which are usually found inconspicuously underneath, have taken on their role. It usually has three leaves, each of which is divided into three parts giving the plant a fragile, lacy look.

Dwarf ginseng, a close relative of the medicinal herb ginseng, looks like the wood anemone in that it has the same three-part leaves, but its flower cluster is made up of tiny white flowers.

The **spring beauty** is another fragile looking ephemeral. It has grasslike leaves and five-petaled flowers that are white to pink with streaks of red.

Yellow trout lily stands out as one of the Island's more attractive native wildflowers. Also referred to as dogtooth violet or adder's tongue, it produces a showy, yellow, six-petaled flower that, not surprisingly, looks like a miniature lily. The leaves are as inconspicuous as the flowers are flamboyant: they look as though they had been sprayed with camouflage paint, being mottled in shades of green and brown. The speckled leaves apparently reminded some ichthyology-minded botanist of the sides of a trout, hence the common name. The yellow trout lily grows in colonies, often containing hundreds of plants. Sterile, immature one-leaved plants which lack flowers are more numerous than the fertile two-leaved individuals.

Trilliums are ostentatious members of the lily family. Three species are native to the Island: red, nodding and painted, each of which has large, three-petaled flowers. Red trillium has, you guessed it, red flowers; nodding displays pale pink flowers; and the painted has white flowers with red veins at the base of each petal.

The grandest splash of spring color, however, belongs to the **marsh marigold.** Like the wood anemone to which it is related, its brilliant inch-and-a-half-wide yellow flowers lack petals; they are made up of showy sepals. Its scientific name, *Caltha palustris*, means "goblet of the swamp," a reference to the gobletlike shape of the flowers and to the habitat which it adorns with such color.

Where To See Spring Wildflowers

SKUNK CABBAGE is one of the most common plants growing on Long Island and can be found in almost all wooded swamps. It is found in **Valley Stream, Hempstead Lake, Connetquot River** and **Caleb Smith State Parks;** the **Tackapausha** and **Massapequa County Preserves;** and **Blydenburgh, Robert C. Murphy** and **Montauk County Parks.**

MARSH MARIGOLD is almost as common as skunk cabbage and can be seen in **Caleb Smith** and **Connetquot River State Parks** and **Blydenburgh County Park.** It is also common in the swamps of **Pelham Bay** and **Van Cortland Parks** just outside our area in the Bronx.

SPRING EPHEMERALS — *wood anemone, yellow trout lily, the trilliums, spring beauty* and *dwarf ginseng* can all be found at the **Shu Swamp** and **Coffin Woods Preserves** maintained by the North Shore Sanctuary, Inc., located in Mill Neck. Spring Beauty is common south of the Alexander Graham Bell School on the very western edge of **Alley Pond Park** in Queens.

Wood anemone and *trout lily* are common at **Montauk County Park** in the damp woods to the south of Big Reed Pond in the area where the nature trail system is located. *Trout lily* also occurs at the **Hoyt Farm Preserve** in Smithtown and on the west side of **Alley Pond Park.** *Wood anemone* is common in **Bill Richards Town Park** in Smithtown, adjacent to Blydenburgh County Park, across from the State Office Building along Route 454.

Key Times

Skunk cabbage — mid-February to early April
Marsh marigold — mid-March to late April
Spring ephemerals — mid-April to early May

CHAPTER TWO

FOWLER'S TOAD. (Robert T. McGrath)

Tigers in the Night

AND OTHER COLD-BLOODED, WET-SKINNED ANIMALS

It was an unseasonably warm night in early February with temperatures in the mid-forties. The last several nights had also been warm, and it had rained heavily the evening before. As the two naturalists loaded up their car with the night's gear — fine mesh nets, flashlights, chest waders and a camera — their thoughts turned to the strange circumstance that motivated them. Here in the middle of winter a cold-blooded animal was stirring: the **eastern tiger salamander.** A member of the genus *Ambystoma*, which includes the group of burrowing amphibians known as the mole salamanders, the tiger salamander (its scientific species name is *tigrinum*) is so named for its orange-yellow and black splotching. It is large in comparison to the other native Long Island mole salamanders — the spotted, blue-spotted and marbled — often reaching a length of eight to ten inches. The Island has four more native salamanders: the northern two-lined, the four-toed, the red-backed and red-spotted newt, but they belong to different genera. The tiger salamander is the first amphibian to emerge in the spring to breed. The males become active first. They burrow up from the spot in the sandy soil where they overwintered, and move down to the breeding pond. In some winters they appear as early as mid-January. Females follow shortly thereafter, and an elaborate courtship behavior begins that includes body-nudging and tail-fanning. (Male tiger salamanders have, when viewed in cross-section, flatter tails than females.)

As in all salamanders, fertilization is internal. The male releases a packet of sperm called a spermatophore that is shaped like a tiny pyramid. The female straddles the packet, enveloping it in her cloaca. Over the next several days she will lay one or more gelatinous egg clusters and anchor them to submerged vegetation or sunken branches. These clusters, each of which contains dozens of eggs, swell to between the size of a golf and tennis ball. The eggs hatch in about one month, and the larvae, which at first have external gills and look like frog tadpoles, reach maturity a few months later.

In New York State, the tiger salamander is now restricted to Long Island, although there are historical records from other locales. It is known to breed in ponds ranging from Nassau County to the South Fork, but the species is concentrated in the Pine Barrens where it prefers small, sandy-bottomed ponds. Given its restricted range and small population, it has been declared an endangered species in New York State.

The **spotted salamander** is the most widespread member of the Ambystoma salamanders and emerges to breed about a month later than the tiger, usually from late March to early April. It is an attractive amphibian with bright yellow dots that look as if they were painted onto a black background. It sometimes forms "breeding congresses," a type of amphibian foreplay, where several dozen salamanders will pack into a tight ball nudging against each other. Its egg mass is larger and firmer than the tiger's.

The **blue-spotted salamander** is the smallest of the Island's mole salamanders, about the size of an adult human's finger. Its Long Island range is restricted to the Montauk peninsula. The species distribution is a classic example of what ecologists call a "disjunct range": the Montauk population's nearest neighbor is on Prince Edward Island, Canada, more than 500 miles away. Its name is derived from the pretty, light blue flecking on its back that has been likened to the enamel cookware of old. The blue-spotted emerges about the same time as the spotted salamander.

The **marbled salamander** rounds out this interesting group of animals, and although it breeds in the fall, it appears here because of its relationship to the other mole salamanders. The marbled is the chunkiest of the four and has white or light blue lines traversing its back, overlaying the dark blue or black body color. The female lays her eggs in moist rather than submerged situations. For example, she may lay under a rotting log at the edge of a vernal (seasonal) pond. She will then guard the eggs until they are covered with water supplied by autumn rains.

About the first of April, as the spotted salamander ambles down to its breeding haunts to create the next generation, it is likely to hear what sounds like the quacking of ducks and the piping of small birds or insects, although none of these animals are about. The "quacking" that resonates from the ponds is the mating chorus of the **wood frog,** a small, handsome frog with a black mask (leading to its two other common names: the bandit and raccoon frog). It is the most terrestrial of our native frogs, spending most of the year foraging in upland areas away from breeding ponds.

The birdlike piping sounds are the amorous serenades of the **spring peeper,** a treefrog species and the smallest amphibian on Long Island. Adults reach only an inch in length. Its species name, *crucifer,* refers to the dark cross on the frog's back.

Next in this amphibious parade is the **Fowler's toad,** the common "hoppity toad" that is often seen in vegetable gardens and back lawns. The Fowler's toad is one of very few animals that may be more abundant today than when Long Island was forest primeval. It has adapted to the use of that common breeding pond found in most suburban housing developments: the recharge basin. From late spring through early summer, the unique call of the Fowler's toad (a blend of whistle and hum) sounds from these basins, as well as natural wetlands throughout Long Island.

Of course there are others: the **leopard frog** with its call that sounds like the animal for which it is named, and the **pickerel frog,** whose call echoes off pond surfaces like the puttering of alien spacecraft. There is the birdlike trilling of the **gray treefrog,** the quintessential "*jug-o-rum*" calls of the **bullfrog** and the song of the **green frog,** reminiscent of a plucked banjo string. Lastly, there is the **spadefoot toad** which waits for the full warmth of summer before snorting its pig-like "*quonk*! *quonk*!" call.

THE RED-BACKED SALAMANDER

The diminutive red-backed or woodland salamander (*Plethedon cinereus*) is one of the more abundant animals on Long Island. In some habitats its population may reach several hundred individuals per square acre, and in certain places this slender four-inch salamander may be the most common animal found. Yet an overwhelming majority of Long Islanders have never seen one. Living a fossorial (adapted for digging) existence, particularly during the day, the red-backed salamander rarely emerges into the open, preferring to spend its time beneath moist rotting logs, or moving about in the thick litter of decomposing leaves.

The prime reason this salamander is so common and widespread has to do with its reproductive habits. Unlike the other amphibians described here, the red-backed salamander is not tied to a pond or wetland in order to reproduce. It lays its eggs in small, discrete clusters beneath moist logs and dense packings of leaves. As a result, the species can populate woodland habitats far from breeding ponds required by other amphibians. Interestingly, the woodland salamander has no lungs with which to respire and hence belongs to a group referred to as the lungless salamanders. It breathes through the mouth lining and through the skin, which must remain moist. This explains why they are rarely seen aboveground where they might easily desiccate.

Two distinct color morphs occur throughout this species' geographical range in the northeastern United States. The typical form is the namesake one: dark gray sides with a dark red dorsal stripe running the length of the body. The other form is the lead-backed phase where the salamander is entirely dark gray. In both forms the ventral side is mottled in a salt-and-pepper effect. Unlike other parts of the species' range where the two morphs intermingle, there is little mixing between the forms on Long Island. Moreover, the abundance of the morphs seems to be habitat-related. The red-backed is more prevalent in moist woodlands dominated by birch, oak and hickory found primarily along the Island's north shore, while the lead-backed phase dominates in drier habitats such as the Pine Barrens found in the central parts of the Island.

A search under logs and thick branches in any of the parks included in this book is bound to turn up individuals of one of the two morphs. Please make sure to roll the log back over into place when you are done to avoid disturbing the micro-community found there and the species that depend upon it. Replace the log before releasing the salamander along its edge, in order to avoid crushing any specimens.

Where To See Salamanders And Frogs

Many of the breeding ponds used by the aforementioned species are isolated and directions would be difficult to give. Furthermore, these species are particularly sensitive during the mating season. Therefore, specific wetland sites are not provided. Rather, you are urged to join others on a field trip scheduled by one of the natural history organizations listed in the appendix.

Key Times

Peak breeding activity for the species, in sequence, is as follows:
Tiger salamander — mid-January to late February
Spotted salamander — late March to early April
Blue-spotted salamander — early to mid-April
Wood frog — late March to early April
Spring peeper — early April through May
Leopard frog — mid- to late April
Pickerel frog — mid-May to early June
Gray treefrog — mid-May to early June
Bull and green frogs — late May to late June
Spadefoot toad — late June to early July

CHAPTER THREE

COMMON TERNS, IMMATURE AND ADULT. (Marc Oliveri)

Plovers, Terns and Skimmers

It is a raw, mid-March day along the barrier beach; a cold, pelting rain is falling, and steady westerly winds cause the rain to feel even colder. Even though the Weather Service reminds us that "March comes in like a lion and goes out like a lamb," spring seems a long way off.

But then you hear it. A pipelike whistle floats down the beach. It sounds again, and you scan; motion catches your eye. Scurrying in the sand about twenty-five yards ahead is a small sand-colored bird: a male piping plover. Suddenly the wind and rain do not matter. If the plovers are returning to their nesting beaches, then spring really cannot be far off.

The **piping plover,** which occurs throughout the eastern United States, is a beach-nesting member of the shorebird family. Nowhere is it doing well. The Great Lakes population has been declared endangered by the United States Fish & Wildlife Service, pursuant to the federal Endangered Species Act, and the northern plains and east coast populations have been listed as threatened. New York also has listed the piping plover as an endangered species, given its critically low numbers in the state. Estimates place the total number at about 2,500 pairs worldwide. About 500 pairs breed on Long Island beaches, making the Island one of the critical areas in the world for this handsome little bird.

The piping plover winters along the Gulf and South Atlantic coasts, but it leaves for its nesting grounds early and is the first of the shorebird group to arrive on Long Island in the spring. Males arrive before females and establish territories. (The sexes are similar in appearance, but the males usually have thicker chest and head bands.) The males show elaborate courtship behavior, such as shell tossing and aerial flight, in their effort to secure a mate.

Once a pair has been formed, four eggs (very rarely three or five), beautifully speckled to aid in their camouflage, are laid in a small depression in the sand that suffices as a nest. Often the nest is decorated with bits of clam shell. Ornithologists first thought the placing of shells in the nest was behavior that strengthened the pair bond, but it is now believed the white shell bits may also serve to reflect heat, thereby keeping the eggs cooler.

After a month of incubation, the eggs hatch and the precocious, down-covered chicks, with eyes wide open, follow their parents in a search for food in the wrack line (the line of natural debris left by high tide) and along the water's edge. They consume a host of food items, including insects and their eggs and larvae, marine worms and small crustaceans. Growing rapidly on this protein-rich diet, the chicks fledge in about three weeks.

Piping plovers nest both singly and in loose colonies, sometimes with six or more nests occurring within a several-hundred-yard stretch of beach. While it breeds on both shores, it is much more common on the south shore barrier beach system. The piping plover prefers the lightly vegetated portions of the upper beach and seems to prefer nesting sites near inlets.

The piping plover shares the Island's sandy and rocky beaches with other nesting birds, sometimes locating their nests within other birds' colonies. Foremost among these others are the black skimmer and the roseate, common and little terns.

The **little tern** is relatively easy to distinguish from the other two breeding terns. As its name indicates, it is small, as a tern goes, and has a bright yellow bill. It has a black cap like the others, but has a white forehead and an easy-to-see black line that runs through the eye. It nests in colonies ranging in size from a few to hundreds of nests, and prefers beaches that have little or no vegetation.

The two bigger terns are more difficult to tell apart, but as well as having different calls, they have field marks that enable their identification. During the breeding season, the bill of the **common tern** is a striking bright red while the roseate's is black with a dull red base. Also, in breeding plumage, the underside of the **roseate tern** is suffused with a pretty light pink which gives the bird its name. The common tern's underside is white. Lastly, the roseate has a longer, more deeply forked tail than the common, a feature especially noticeable in flight.

These birds also may breed in colonies together, the common tern preferring to place its nest amid scattered clumps of beach grass and seaside goldenrod, and the roseate tern selecting the more heavily vegetated areas of the upper beach.

The **black skimmer,** one of the more distinctive birds found on Long Island, would be hard to confuse with anything else. The bird is also known as "cutwater" due to its famous habit of fishing by trailing its lower mandible in the water and snapping its bill closed on any fish it encounters. In fact, the behavior is so ingrained in the bird that the lower mandible grows twice as fast as the upper one to compensate for wear. On Long Island, skimmers nest in or along the edges of little or common tern colonies.

The skimmer has a unique call that is similar to a dog barking. When several birds call as they fly by, it sounds like a pack of dogs in hot pursuit of some unfortunate quarry.

The two larger terns and the black skimmer leave their wintering grounds in the northern part of South America or the Caribbean in late winter, reaching Long Island by late April to early May.

Unfortunately, these waterbirds, like the piping plover, are not doing well. The roseate tern is listed as endangered by the federal and New York State governments, the little as threatened by the federal government and endangered by the State, and the common as a threatened species by the State. Although not classified as endangered, skimmers probably should be since there are probably less than a thousand found in New York.

These fascinating birds face an array of threats that affect their reproductive success. Coastal habitat is highly desirable for vacation homes and marinas, and as more of it becomes converted to these and other uses, less is available for the birds. Also, coastal habitats are intensively used for recreational activities, such as swimming, off-road-vehicle use, camping and fishing. All these activities have a negative impact on the birds. Moreover, the coast is a dynamic environment that can change quickly, sometimes within a couple of days or weeks. Nesting birds may find themselves in the unenviable position of having a nesting area destroyed and being unable to locate an alternate site, due to competing uses in the coastal zone. Also, the habitat these birds use is successional, meaning that vegetation there will become more extensive through time, rendering the habitat unusable to the birds if it is not periodically reduced. This task always seems to be low on the scale of priorities for public beach managers.

THE LONG ISLAND COLONIAL WATERBIRD ASSOCIATION

Recognizing that plovers, terns, skimmers and other waterbirds face an array of threats, a loosely knit umbrella organization known as the Long Island Colonial Waterbird Association (LICWA) was formed in the mid-1980s to develop strategies to more effectively protect and manage these birds.

The organization consists of individuals and agencies concerned about the future of these birds and includes the United States Fish and Wildlife Service, New York State Department of Environmental Conservation, The Nature Conservancy, National Audubon Society, Suffolk County Parks Department, Seatuck Research Program and many others.

Members of LICWA do much to help these birds. An annual island-wide census is conducted to determine species trends. Through tern stewards hired by The Nature Conservancy's Long Island chapter with funding support from the State's Return-A-Gift-to-Wildlife program, bird colonies are fenced, posted and patrolled in an effort to minimize vandalism and disturbance. A slide lecture on the life history and threats to these birds is available to interested groups.

If you would like to make a tangible contribution toward helping the Island's wildlife, call the New York Department of Environmental Conservation at (516) 444-0305, the Long Island Chapter of The Nature Conservancy at (516) 367-3225, or the South Fork-Shelter Island office of the Conservancy at (516) 725-2936 to find out how you can become a volunteer tern warden.

Where To See Plovers, Terns & Skimmers

There are more than 150 sites on Long Island where piping plovers, black skimmers or little, roseate and common terns nest. After the breeding season the birds disperse and may be seen virtually anywhere in the coastal zone. At that time of year, the inlets are usually reliable locations to view terns.

IT IS VITAL TO THE BREEDING SUCCESS OF THESE ENDANGERED BIRDS THAT THEY NOT BE DISTURBED IN ANY WAY. YOU ARE URGED TO EXERCISE GOOD JUDGMENT AND REMAIN A SUFFICIENT DISTANCE FROM COLONIES TO AVOID DISTURBING OR HARASSING BIRDS.

Breezy Point Cooperative — extreme southwestern Queens.

Silver Point Park — Hempstead, adjacent to East Rockaway.

Jones Beach State Park — West End and Short Beach sections; also adjacent to parking field #9.

Cedar and **Overlook Beach** — Babylon. Cedar Beach common tern colony is one of the largest in the northeast. More than 13,000 birds nested here in 1985. There is so much activity that many birds can be seen from the beach parking lot.

Sand City/Eaton's Neck — Huntington, the southwestern tip of the Neck is a town park called Sand City.

Young's Island/Stony Brook Harbor — Brookhaven. A good vantage point is at Stony Brook Yacht Club across Porpoise Channel.

Shirley Marina — Brookhaven. The site is on west side of William Floyd Parkway immediately north of the bay.

Roe Avenue — Patchogue. On the east side at its terminus with the bay.

Cupsogue County Park — Southampton. A number of ocean sites from here east to Shinnecock Inlet.

Shinnecock East County Park — Southampton.

Cedar Point County Park — East Hampton.

Cedar Beach County Park — Southold.

Key Times

Piping plover — Arrive by mid-March, depart by early September

Little, common and **roseate terns** — Arrive by early May, depart by mid- to late September

Black skimmers — Arrive by early to mid-May, depart by mid-September.

AMERICAN WOODCOCK. (Marc Oliveri)

CHAPTER FOUR

Flight of the Woodcock

OR THINGS THAT GO "PEENT" IN THE NIGHT

The **American woodcock,** often referred to simply as the woodcock, or more colorfully as the timberdoodle or mud bat, is certainly one of the Island's more unusual native birds.

It is a chunky, squat bird, seemingly too fat for its own good. Its head seems too small for its body, and its bill too large for its head. Its eyes are placed past the middle position on the sides of the head, so the woodcock, it could be said, truly has eyes in the back of his head. (Not a bad place to have your eyes if you spend a lot of time with your bill in the ground as the woodcock does.) To its credit, the bird is wonderfully camouflaged; it looks like a pile of leaves on the forest floor, its preferred habitat.

The woodcock is a member of the shorebird family, a large family of birds that includes sandpipers, plovers, godwits, et cetera (see Chapters 3 and 18). Its closest relative in the family is the common snipe. But unlike these other species that frequent the shore, the woodcock, as its name suggests, is right at home in the woods, particularly in moist, heavily wooded thickets.

The bill of the woodcock is two-and-a-half to three inches long and is highly sensitive. It is used to probe in the soil for earthworms which make up the bulk of the bird's diet. (It has been reported that a woodcock will eat more than its weight in earthworms daily.) In fact, the tip of the top mandible is flexible so when the bird encounters a worm, it closes on it in forceps-like fashion. Woodcock are known to share feeding grounds, which can sometimes be located by "poke holes" scattered about an area.

The woodcock is not restricted to woodland habitats. It often feeds in rich, moist thickets and along the edges of streams and fields. It nests in second growth forest, and uses overgrown fields for courtship displays.

These spring displays, beginning in mid-February and continuing to late April, occur a half-hour or so before dawn when the sky is turning from black to violet, at crepuscule (late dusk) and on moonlit nights. The bird seems to cue on a particular light intensity.

A male struts in front of a prospective mate and begins to make a "*peent*" sound. It takes off, spiraling upward into the sky, continuing to peent as it goes. Three modified flight feathers make a twittering sound as the bird continues to climb. At the height of the flight (often several hundred feet) it emits a bubbly, twittering song and plunges to earth. Air rushing through the flight feathers during the downward plunge causes them to make a loud warbling sound. This behavior is repeated many times during the course of a night.

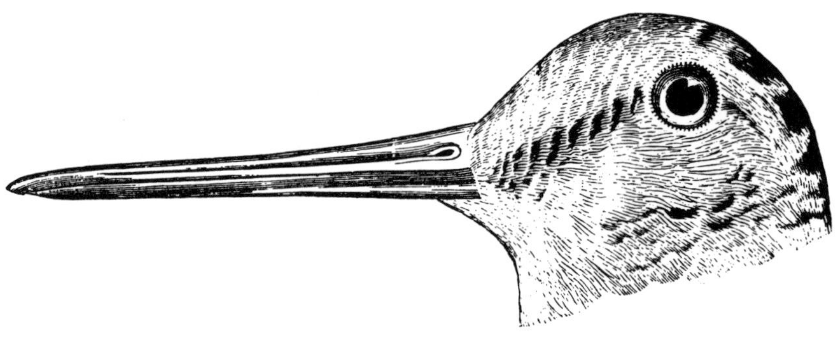

AMERICAN WOODCOCK, *actual size*. (From *The Water Birds of North America,* by Baird, Brewer, Ridgway)

Where To See Woodcock Courtship Displays

Although the woodcock is declining, there still exist a number of locations in Nassau and Suffolk Counties to view the courtship display. However, given the importance of the display to the bird's reproductive success, specific sites are not listed. Instead, consult with the natural history organizations listed in the back of the book and join one of the many group walks scheduled each spring to watch the display.

Key Times

The courtship display can be seen from mid-February to early May at dawn or dusk. Woodcock can also be seen, most often when they have been flushed, from early spring through late November.

OSPREYS. (Robert T. McGrath)

CHAPTER FIVE

The Osprey's Return

If Long Islanders were asked to choose a bird that symbolizes the essence of the Island, the **osprey** would be the probable winner. After all, the osprey frequents the very areas — the bays, harbors and ocean coastline — that make the Island such a special place to live. Here in its estuarine domain, it is the most impressive bird to be seen with its five-foot wingspan, attractive brown and white plumage, bright yellow eyes, shiny black talons and spectacular fishing plunges from more than 100 feet.

Long Island has long been home to the osprey, or fish hawk as it is also known due to its obligatory diet of fish. As recently as the 1930s, the east end of Long Island possessed one of the greatest concentrations of osprey nests in the world. For example, several hundred nests were found on Gardiner's Island (situated between the two forks in Gardiner's Bay), making it the largest known colony in the world, and only slightly fewer nests were found at Plum Island (off the tip of Orient Point) a few decades before.

Between 1950 and 1975 the osprey went into serious decline. The Gardiner's Island population slid to a mere twenty-five nesting pairs. Some estimates suggested that southern New England and Long Island osprey populations decreased by ninety percent during this time. Ferreting out the cause of the decline was one of this nation's most interesting wildlife detective stories. Was it illegal hunting or destruction of coastal habitat? What about scarcity of the fish species they depended upon? The magnitude of the geographic area affected, however, suggested some other cause. Pollution might be a possibility, given that pollutants can spread over large areas rather quickly.

As it turned out, the problem sprang from a particular type of contaminant, DDT, a persistent pesticide that was in widespread use during this time to control mosquitoes and crop pests. Due primarily to run-off from the land, a variety of fish species became contaminated. Through them, the pesticide, fat-soluble and not easily excreted, built up in the birds' fatty tissues. While there were a few reports of adults dying directly from lethal residue levels in their bodies, the drop-off had more to do with the inability of affected birds to lay viable eggs, and therefore to produce a new generation of ospreys.

Biochemists learned that the pesticide interfered with the birds' ability to metabolize the calcium needed for making eggshells. As a result, many eggs had shells which were too thin, and they cracked during incubation, killing the embryos. In several recorded cases eggs were laid without shells at all. Many other bird species also were affected by DDT, including bald eagles, peregrine falcons and brown pelicans.

In 1972, alarmed by what was happening, concerned Long Island scientists brought legal action in an effort to stop the Suffolk County Mosquito Commission from using DDT. (This group went on to form the Environmental Defense Fund, a well-respected national environmental organization dealing with such issues as global warming, acid rain, solid waste and ozone depletion.) Successful legal action resulted in the pesticide's discontinuance. Flushed with victory, the group moved to have it banned nationally and, following several court decisions, was successful there too.

With DDT banned, osprey numbers slowly began to climb. During the 1980s, the number of breeding pairs rose, and their range began to expand westward. Today, there are several nesting pairs in Nassau County, and recently the bird returned to New York City. In 1992, Long Island had 226 active nests which produced a total of 260 young. The fish hawk is not out of the woods, though, and is still listed as a threatened species in New York.

Flying north from their wintering grounds, which range from the southeastern United States, the Caribbean and northern South America, the osprey predictably reappears on Long Island within a three- to five-day period in mid-March (17th-21st), with males usually arriving first. It is thought that established pairs return to the same nest site used the year before. New mates establish new nests.

Osprey nests are a thing of legend. Made from dead, interwoven branches of various sizes, which the adults scavenge or pluck from trees, the nests can be three to four feet deep, six feet across and weigh several hundred pounds. Those which survive the gusts of winter are embellished each year and grow bigger and bigger. The cup can be more than a foot-and-a-half deep, making it difficult to see an incubating bird. The nest's large size and conspicuous placement makes the osprey among the easiest of birds to census.

Ospreys will use a variety of items to support nests. Large, flat-topped trees are preferred, but trees with the right configuration and size are in short supply. These adaptable birds often use human-made structures such as utility poles, fence posts, light stanchions and channel markers. A pair of fish hawks nested for several years atop a light tower illuminating a race track in central Suffolk County. On Robin's Island, situated in the middle of Peconic Bay, one pair of ospreys have a nest atop a large glacial boulder that sits in shallow water about fifty yards from shore; another rests atop an old duck blind and still another resided for several decades on a small storage building attached to the main dock.

Ospreys will readily take to a nesting platform made from an old wagon wheel or crosshatched two-by-fours. A few attached starter branches and a perch branch are important embellishments. Cone-shaped collars are placed on the pole to prevent predation of the eggs or young. Over the past five years, dozens of platforms have been erected in suitable coastal habitat throughout Long Island with the hope of attracting nesting ospreys. "Platform raisings" have become a popular annual activity for several Long Island environmental organizations.

Like the proverbial packrat (and many people for that matter), ospreys seem to like to collect things. Clothing, rubber boots, fishing net, rope, dolls and assorted other objects have been found in association with their nests.

A fish hawk is well adapted to hunting for fish. Its oily plumage helps to repel water, which is an important adaptation for a bird that is regularly submerged. It takes many dives before the plumage becomes waterlogged, requiring the bird to sit with wings extended, waiting for them to dry.

The bird possesses four very sharp, curved talons on each foot that can snap shut in as little as one-fiftieth of a second. The outer toe is flexible and can be moved to become opposable. This enables the bird to grasp a fish more securely, with two toes forward and two toes back in parrot fashion (instead of three forward and one back). Also, the skin of the foot and the base of the toes is covered with short, rough spines, called spicules, that aid in gripping fish. Moreover, ospreys are long-legged, enabling them to reach deep into the water for fish.

Herring, menhaden and, in shallow water, flounder are all prey for ospreys. Once caught, the fish is carried back to the nest headfirst to minimize wind resistance.

Long Island ospreys characteristically lay three eggs (range two to four) and both sexes incubate for the 32-33 days it takes for the eggs to hatch. The young fledge in approximately two months. The fledged young can be distinguished from the adults by the abundance of light-colored speckling on the brown back. Most juveniles and adults move south by mid-October, and by early November are rare. If you live near an active nest, it can be fun to guess the arrival and departure dates of "your" ospreys, with the winner, of course, being treated to a delicious seafood dinner.

OSPREY EGG, *actual size.* (From *Life Histories of North American Birds,* by Bendire)

BALD EAGLES ON LONG ISLAND

I have known them to appear in flocks of 15-20 on the marshes near the sea coast on Long Island, after a violent northeast storm. The inhabitants, on such occasions, approach them on horseback, and after killing many outright, dispatch the remaining wounded ones with clubs.

— JAMES E. DEKAY, 1843

The "them" DeKay was eloquently describing were bald eagles, perhaps the most majestic birds in North America. The eagle once built its huge stick nests on Long Island and was a regular winter visitor. Supporting DeKay's observations, Jacob Giraud, who wrote the first book on Long Island's birdlife in 1844, reported winters in which sixty or seventy bald eagles were killed. These incidents of persecution, and the fact that eagles, unlike ospreys, require undisturbed nesting sites (an increasingly rare commodity as Long Island developed), led to the species' decline and eventual extirpation from the Island. The last recorded nest on Long Island was in 1930 on Gardiner's Island, which had one of the world's largest colonies of ospreys during this time.

Eagles, like ospreys, are recovering from the effects of DDT in some parts of their east coast range (Maine, Chesapeake Bay, Florida Everglades), but they have yet to recolonize heavily developed areas such as Long Island.

Nowadays, bald eagles are occasionally seen on Long Island, though, so keep your eyes on the sky. They are sometimes reported during the summer, but more often during the fall when they are migrating, and in the winter when they appear as temporary visitors. Both adults and immature birds (lacking the white or "bald" heads) are seen.

The best time and location to see bald eagles in New York State is from December through March at the Swinging Bridge, Mongaup and Rio Reservoir complex in upstate Sullivan County, about five miles west/southwest of Monticello. These sites are approximately three hours away by car from western Long Island.

Where To See Ospreys

With some luck ospreys can be encountered on just about any visit to the seashore from April to September. They can be seen flying to and from nests, or, if you are particularly lucky, plunging for fish. By standing an appropriate distance from an active nest or near a known fishing spot, you may be able to view incubating adults, adults returning with fish, or perhaps fledgling young.

DO NOT APPROACH ANY CLOSER THAN 150 YARDS FROM AN ACTIVE NEST. DOING SO MAY DISTURB THE BIRDS AND COULD RESULT IN CHICK MORTALITY. ALSO, THE ADULTS MAY VIEW YOU AS AN INTRUDER AND DIVE-BOMB. ON RARE OCCASIONS, THEY HAVE BEEN KNOWN TO RAKE PEOPLE'S HEADS WITH THEIR TALONS!

Active nests are scattered throughout Long Island; some can be found at the following locations:

Cedar Beach County Park — Southold
Cedar Point County Park — East Hampton
Connetquot River State Park Preserve — Oakdale
Goldsmith's Inlet County Park — Peconic
Hubbard County Park — Flanders
Mashomack Preserve — The Nature Conservancy, Shelter Island
Morton National Wildlife Refuge — Noyac
Northwest Harbor County Park — East Hampton
Orient Point Causeway (including Hashomomack Pond) — Orient

Ram Island Causeway — Shelter Island
Robin's and **Gardiner's Islands**
Terrells River County Park — Center Moriches
Wertheim National Wildlife Refuge — Shirley

Key Times

Late March: Ospreys arrive
Late October: Ospreys depart

CHAPTER SIX

ALEWIFE STREAM IN NORTH SEA. (John L. Turner)

The Run of the Alewife

Even if less appreciated and understood, the migratory movements of fish are no less impressive than the more fabled navigational feats of birds. Anadromous fish, which spawn in freshwater and mature in salt, move from natal streams (streams of birth) to developmental areas and back with remarkable precision. The **alewife** serves as an excellent example.

In early spring, schools of alewives move in from open ocean waters to shallower coastal areas. Once these waters warm enough, usually mid-April to mid-May on Long Island, the fish move into position at the mouth of their natal stream. Although the cues they use to do so are still poorly understood, some scientists hypothesize that the distinct "odor fingerprint" of each stream is a factor. Then, through a triggering mechanism that is also poorly understood, they move *en masse* up the stream. The "run" has begun. Those females that avoid the nets of people and the beaks of night herons to reach their spawning grounds, each deposit up to a quarter of a million eggs. When spawning is complete, the fish reverse themselves and head for coastal waters.

Alewife eggs hatch within three to seven days, depending on water temperature. Developing rapidly, the fingerlings grow to three to four inches by September or October when they leave their natal stream or pond, destined for the open sea.

Adult alewives reach a length of fifteen to eighteen inches and have pearly-silver sides and a greenish colored back. They are distinctive in having deeply forked tails, large caudal (back) fins and large, prominent black eyes.

The alewife is a member of the herring family and is closely related to the shad, a fish which is seeing a resurgence in the Hudson and Connecticut Rivers. Caught as they migrate upstream to spawn, the shad (and its roe) are the focus of a number of food festivals sponsored each May in towns along both sides of the Hudson River.

Two hundred years ago the start of an alewife run would have been met with much excitement and the cry "the herring are running!" The alewife was an important resource to colonial America. In Massachusetts some of the earliest laws to protect and regulate wildlife were enacted to safeguard the fish. The first such law, enacted in 1709 stated, "That no wears [weirs], hedges, fishgarths, kiddles, or other disturbance or encumbrance shall be set, erected or made, on or across any river, to the stopping, obstructing, or straitening of the natural or usual course and passage of the fish in their seasons, or spring of the year, without the approbation and allowance first had and obtained from the general sessions of the peace in the same county...." This law was followed by another in 1741 which was enacted to "prevent the destruction of the fish called alewives, and other fish."

Being a rather bony fish, the alewife was used during colonial times as much for fertilizer as for food. They were dumped by the thousands in corn fields and apparently were such a good source of nutrients that the townspeople could distinguish "fish corn" from regular corn. This practice was made illegal when folk came to realize alewife stocks were declining.

Alewives have not only declined due to overharvesting. On Long Island, where there is no evidence that alewives were harvested to the point of decline, their status has, nevertheless, changed markedly for the worst: from alewife runs in several dozen Long Island streams to about half a dozen runs today. The overwhelming culprit has proven to be dams and other obstructions that prevent the fish from reaching their freshwater spawning grounds.

Yet through the installation of fish ladders — stepped pathways that circumvent the dam, connecting the upper and lower parts of the waterbody — fish can gain access to important, previously inaccessible headwaters. The prevalence of such ladders in Massachusetts streams is one reason why many alewife runs there remain intact (twenty-four on Cape Cod alone). Unfortunately, on Long Island there has been little interest on the part of the State Department of Environmental Conservation in requiring or encouraging their installation.

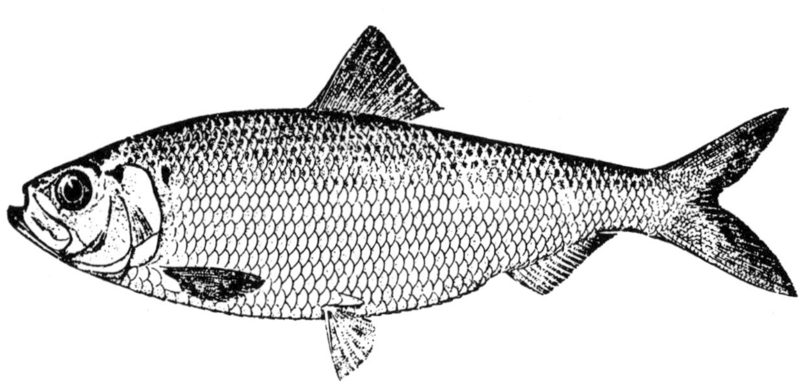

ALEWIFE. (From *Fishes of the Gulf of Maine,* by Bigelow and Schroeder)

SHADBUSH IN FLOWER, JUNEBERRY IN FRUIT

Out of necessity, early settlers saw connections between elements of the natural world. They understood the relationships between, and among, plants and animals, and the influence of soil and weather on both. Much of this "earth wisdom" has taken on a folklorish quality today, and people generally have discounted its importance, though, in truth, they are no less dependent upon it.

An example of a connection made is the shadbush. A small tree with handsome gray bark, shadbush sends forth its sprays of white, five-petaled flowers in the spring at the same time that shad and alewife ascend their natal streams to spawn. Settlers therefore had showy banners to remind them of the arrival of an important food source.

As the alternate name, Juneberry, indicates, the sweet berries ripen in late June. Those spared by birds and animals were made into jams, jellies and pies.

Shadbush is common on Long Island, particularly on the South Fork and Montauk peninsula. It is prevalent at **Montauk County Park** and **Montauk State Park.** It is also common at **Northwest Harbor** and **Cedar Point County Parks.**

Where To See Alewives

There are about half a dozen known alewife runs remaining on Long Island, but by far the most observable run is located in the community of North Sea and involves the unnamed stream connecting Big Fresh Pond and North Sea Harbor, crossing under Noyac and North Sea Roads in the process. Park on the side of Noyac Road about one hundred yards east of where it breaks off from North Sea Road, making sure to pay attention to existing "No Parking" signs.

Given the elevational difference in the stream due to the culvert running underneath Noyac Road, it is best to time your visit with high tide. It is only then that the water is high enough for the fish to gain access to the culvert and move upstream. If you arrive at any other time, you may see a few fish that entered the stream on the previous high tide and are waiting for the boost of the next tide. You may also see the remains of dead fish that night herons and other predators have fed upon.

The point where the stream passes beneath North Sea Road is also a good vantage point, but is not recommended because of the lack of parking space on the road's shoulder.

Key Times

During high tides from about April 10 through the first week of May.

CHAPTER SEVEN

HIGHBUSH BLUEBERRY. (Robert T. McGrath)

Blueberries

BLUE TONGUES FOR EVERYONE

There are several groups of plants that are particularly well represented on Long Island, and the blueberry or heath family (*Ericaceae*), with more than two dozen native species, is one such example. The group is most common in the Pine Barrens where at least eighteen of the twenty-six species find the droughty, acidic soil conditions to their liking. In fact, it is possible to stand in some places in the Pine Barrens and identify six or seven members of the family.

With a group this large it is impossible to describe each species. It would not be worthwhile anyway, since a few are so closely related that a nontechnical writing would not be helpful in distinguishing them. Representative species are discussed instead. It is fun to try to identify all the members of a group (that is what keeps many bird watchers going) so why not give it a shot with the native members of the blueberry family?

One of the more well-known members of the group is **trailing arbutus** (*Epigaea repens*), a plant which illustrates the value of learning a species' scientific or Latin name. People are often frightened of these seemingly hard-to-pronounce names, despite the fact they use Latin names all the time — chrysanthemum, being just one example. With the trailing arbutus, the prefix, *epi-*, means "upon," the suffix, *-gaea*, means "the earth," so the generic name literally means "upon the earth." The species name, *repens*, (think of what physical position you might be in if you are repenting) means to lie flat or trail. Accordingly, the full meaning of the scientific name means to "trail upon the earth", a precise reference to the growth habit of this attractive little plant. Learning the meaning of a species' Latin name can often enhance your appreciation of its nature or character.

Trailing arbutus, also known as mayflower, has leathery oval leaves that form small ground cover mats. The flowers, blooming in late April, range from white to pink and are shaped like little trumpets with the tube flaring outward to form five petals. Arbutus flowers are varyingly fragrant, some emitting a strong, spicy fragrance, others releasing a more delicate, perfumy scent. Trailing arbutus is almost always found along trail banks or road cuts, only rarely growing in wooded openings. A mat or two of arbutus cascading down a slope is one of the prettier confirmations of spring.

Bearberry is another ground-hugging member of the blueberry family. Requiring direct sunlight, it is restricted to openings and clearings which are often the result of disturbance. With its attractive, shiny dark-green leaves, it creates large sprawling mats that can encompass hundreds of square feet in appropriate pine barrens habitat.

Bearberry produces typical blueberry flowers: small bell-shaped flowers that grow together in small to large clusters. Like the trailing arbutus, it blossoms in late April. If pollinated, the flowers evolve into pretty scarlet red berries that give the plant a Christmas-like look in July. Though not poisonous, the fruit is not really edible either. Its consistency gives new meaning to the word "mealy," somewhat akin to eating a ball of cotton.

Two other low stature heaths are the spotted and striped wintergreens. **Spotted wintergreen** has small, round, dark green leaves and produces a small cluster of bell-shaped flowers which become bright red berries when mature. These berries, however, have a pleasant taste made famous by various wintergreen candies. **Striped wintergreen,** in contrast, has toothed, elongated leaves with a stripe running down the middle. Its waxy looking flowers have five petals with prominent stamens which produce a woody, inedible fruit. Striped wintergreen is closely related to *pipsissewa*, or prince's pine, another heath common on Long Island.

The genus *Vaccinium* contains the "true" blueberries and includes two species of **lowbush blueberries** that are prevalent members of the shrub layer in many pine barrens communities. The berries are small, but sweet. The juiciest berries, however, belong to the two species of **highbush blueberries,** one of which produces a blue blueberry, the other produces a black blueberry. Reaching six to ten feet high in moist soil conditions, these highbush blueberries produce sweet, fingernail-sized berries and are the source from which the commercially important blueberry cultivars were developed.

Related to the blueberries are the **huckleberries.** Of this group, black huckleberry, with its sweet, but seedy, black fruits and brilliant scarlet leaves in autumn, is the most common. Its cousin, the **dangleberry,** so named because of the long stalks from which the individual berries hang, is locally common.

Surprisingly, the two native laurels — mountain and sheep laurel — are members of the blueberry family. **Sheep laurel** is common throughout the Pine Barrens, and while scattered clumps of mountain laurel are found there as well, it is more common in oak-dominated forests. Both display showy flowers. The **mountain laurel** has large clusters of light pink blossoms protruding from the ends of branches, and the smaller sheep laurel (so named because its foliage is poisonous to sheep and other livestock) has a cluster of darker pink flowers that form below the ends of the leaves. Mountain laurel often forms dense impenetrable stands, and when in flower in late spring, these thickets paint the entire understory in hues of pale pink.

There are several blueberry species that grow in standing water or waterlogged soils. These include **fetterbush, maleberry,** and **swamp**

azalea, all of which are locally common constituents of wooded swamp communities in the Pine Barrens. Swamp azalea stands out in the spring with its showy (and sticky), fragrant, white flowers, and during the winter with its large flower buds.

Leatherleaf is a smaller shrub that forms dense, waist-high stands in bogs and along streams. It is so named because of its tough, leathery leaves which have rust-colored spots on their undersides. This heath family member produces pretty, one-sided clusters of bell-shaped flowers known as racemes. Flowering in mid- to late April, it is a sure sign that spring has arrived in the wetlands, and that sunning turtles cannot be far behind.

Where To See Blueberries

As mentioned above many blueberry species are quite common while others have a more local distribution.

Trailing arbutus — common along trails throughout the Pine Barrens including those in the **Manorville Hills, Riverhead Hills,** parts of **Robert C. Murphy County Park,** and particularly in the Suffolk County-owned **Maple Swamp** property in Flanders. It is also common in the southern section of **West Hills County Park** located in Huntington.

Bearberry — widespread throughout the Pine Barrens including the Dwarf Pine Plains. It is abundant along the shoulders of State Route 24 (Exit 71 of the Long Island Expressway) and along the eastern shoulder of Nicholl's Road (County Route 97), just north of its intersection with Route 347. It occurs along the broken-up asphalt road that leads into **Cranberry Bog County Nature Preserve** in Riverhead. It is also abundant at Suffolk County's **Birch Creek/Owl Pond Preserve** in Flanders.

SPOTTED WINTERGREEN, LOWBUSH BLUEBERRIES, BLACK HUCKLEBERRY — common in the Dwarf Pine Plains, the southern end of **Robert C. Murphy County Park, Maple Swamp, Brookhaven State Park, The Rocky Point Management Area** and the **Edgewood State Preserve.**

STRIPED WINTERGREEN — common in all the areas mentioned above except the Dwarf Pine Plains; it is also common in **Blydenburgh County Park.**

HIGHBUSH BLUEBERRIES — found in a large number of places including **Robert C. Murphy County Park** adjacent to the former cranberry bog, also the southern section of the park near Brookhaven National laboratory, **Hubbard County Park,** and in the woods on the west side of the western section of **Cathedral Pines County Park.** It also occurs in **Cunningham Park** in Queens.

SHEEP LAUREL — found in the **Manorville Hills, Riverhead Hills, San Soucci County Nature Preserve, Sears-Bellows County Park** and **Maple Swamp.**

MOUNTAIN LAUREL — abundant at **West Hills County Park** in Huntington, particularly the section on the west side of Sweet Hollow Road and south of Northern State Parkway and the main section of the park on the east side of Sweet Hollow Road, north of Northern State Parkway. It is also in the woods along the eastbound lanes of the Northern State Parkway between exits 42 and 43. It is common in several north shore preserves owned by the Long Island Chapter of The Nature Conservancy, such as the **Butler-Huntington Woods**

Preserve in Smithtown and **St. John's Pond Sanctuary,** and is abundant at the State's **Planting Fields Arboretum** in Upper Brookville.

FETTERBUSH, MALEBERRY, SWAMP AZALEA, LEATHERLEAF — found at **Robert C. Murphy County Park** and the **Quogue Wildlife Refuge.** Leatherleaf is also common at **Owl Pond** on the west side of Spinney Road, west of Sears-Bellows County Park.

Key Times (Flowers)

TRAILING ARBUTUS — mid-April to early May
BEARBERRY — mid-April to early May
WINTERGREENS — Early June through mid-July
BLUEBERRIES, HUCKLEBERRIES — early May though early June
LAURELS — early to late June
FETTERBUSH — late June through early July
MALEBERRY — mid-June through mid-July
SWAMP AZALEA — late June through late July
LEATHERLEAF — mid-April to early May

Key Times (Berries)

BLUEBERRIES appear from mid-June to late July.

CHAPTER EIGHT

HERMIT THRUSH. (Marc Oliveri)

Songbird Migration

To many people the defining event of spring is the northerly migration of hundreds of millions of birds, involving several hundred species, from their tropical and subtropical wintering grounds to their summer breeding territories. While this group includes previously mentioned birds such as the piping plover, osprey and woodcock, the essence of spring migration is the movement of songbirds during the last week of April and the first three weeks of May.

Located midway along the Atlantic coast, Long Island represents a brief sojourn for some birds who are passing through, headed for more northerly destinations. For others, however, the Island is the end of the annual spring journey. It is here they will nest.

Remember the saying "the early bird gets the worm?" To be accurate for birds in an ecological sense, the adage must be amended to "the early bird gets the worm if there are worms about; otherwise, it starves to death." While the point may seem awkward, this situation is what most migratory, insect-eating songbirds confront in the spring.

The timing of arrival on the spring nesting grounds is a balance of good and evil from the birds' point of view. On one side is the benefit derived from arriving early: early birds are able to pick the best breeding sites, thereby enhancing their likelihood of reproductive success. On the other side is the threat of several days of inclement weather, often realized in northern latitudes in early spring. Insect prey, in that case, will be decimated, and many a bird will starve to death. So there we have it: arrive too early and you risk death by starvation, arrive too late and you lose out on the best breeding sites. Such is the life of a songbird in the spring.

Still, spring migration is a more compressed affair than its fall counterpart due to the reproductive urge of the birds and the desire to secure optimal breeding sites. As a result, songbirds move through more quickly in the spring than in the fall. The best flights occur after a high pressure system has passed, but before a low pressure system associated with a cold front has moved in. These conditions result in a northerly flow of warmer air from the south, creating the tailwind songbirds like to take advantage of.

The warblers, often referred to as the "butterflies of the bird world" because of their bright colors and flitting, active movements, are many birders' favorite songbirds. To catch a "wave" of migratory warblers as they dart about the treetops, through the understory or on the ground, all the while singing their pretty and distinctive songs, is to experience the highlight of the spring season.

Thirty-nine species (or thirty-eight if the Bachman's warbler has become extinct) occur in the eastern United States, and thirty-seven of them pass through Long Island at least occasionally. Twenty-one warblers have bred or currently breed here. Common species include the yellow warbler (whose call sounds like "*sweet, sweet, I'm so sweet*"), the yellowthroat ("*witchity, witchity, witchity*"), the ovenbird ("*teacher, teacher, teacher*"), American redstart (a short to-the-point song that drops off at the end), pine warbler (a steady insect-like trill) and prairie warbler (a buzz that goes up the musical scale, somewhat akin to the sound made when a glass is filled with water).

There are, of course, a host of other colorful songbirds that pass through or nest in suitable habitat on Long Island. A few examples include:

- scarlet tanager — a breeder in dry woodlands;
- rose-breasted grosbeak — in moist woodlands and at the edges of wetlands;
- northern oriole (formerly the Baltimore oriole) — in suburban settings and along streams and roads;
- indigo bunting — in second growth forests and old field habitats;
- cedar waxwing — so named because of the brilliantly colored wing tips that look as if they were dipped in hot wax; nests along the edges of fields;
- eastern bluebird — in open fields and Pine Barrens; and
- wood thrush — with its beautiful and haunting songs at dusk that carry through the thick forest where it nests.

This brief list hardly does justice to the myriad songbirds to be seen on Long Island. To give a better estimation, we should mention the flycatchers, including the eastern phoebe and wood pewee; vireos; kinglets; wrens; nuthatches; chickadees and titmice; the robin and other thrushes, including the hermit thrush, Walt Whitman's favorite bird; nearly a dozen sparrow species; bobolinks and meadowlarks frequenting open grassland areas; cardinals; catbirds and mockingbirds; crossbills, with their uniquely shaped bills used to extract seeds; and the American goldfinch.

Add to this impressive list of songbirds the non-perching birds — waterfowl, birds-of-prey, wading birds, shorebirds, terns, gulls and woodpeckers — and you quickly see why Long Island is a mecca for the bird watcher.

Neotropical Migrants

The term neotropical migrant is a fancy name for a bird that seasonally migrates between North America and Central or South America. Some examples of the several hundred species of neotropical migrants that breed in North America are:

- warbling vireo
- American redstart
- blackpoll warbler
- indigo bunting
- magnolia warbler
- ovenbird
- prairie warbler
- scarlet tanager
- northern oriole
- whip-poor-will
- common nighthawk
- eastern kingbird
- least flycatcher
- wood pewee
- veery
- wood thrush
- black-billed cuckoo
- bobolink

Neotropical migrants have received a great deal of attention from the scientific community and general public over the past few years due to their declining abundance. Some species show chronic decline, others acute; estimates range from less than one percent to as much as five percent annually. Birds declining at the faster rate would find their numbers cut in half in as little as a decade.

Various studies document this decline. The Breeding Bird Survey, begun in 1965 by the United States Fish & Wildlife Service, is a nationwide survey conducted during the breeding season. It was designed to discern population trends in bird species and provides the most comprehensive data base for this use.

More imaginative studies have involved the use of weather radar along the Gulf coast to determine migrant concentrations crossing the Gulf of Mexico. More imaginative still are estimates based on the number of birds flying in front of the full moon.

Shrinking migratory populations have been noticed by birders as well, particularly those who have been involved in the avocation for many years. They remember the good old days when spring migration was characterized by wave after wave of warblers and was chock-full of other birds for days on end. Today, these waves occasionally occur, but not in the numbers they once did.

Although many specifics have not yet been worked out, the cause for this alarming decline has become clear. Large expanses of the forests upon which these birds depend are being cleared and/or fragmented at significant rates. This is happening on both breeding and wintering grounds, placing the birds in double jeopardy.

The impact of clearing on wintering grounds is probably more significant, since the total wintering area used by these birds is much smaller than the total breeding area. For example, the United States and forested Canada (the breeding grounds) contain about forty million acres of land. In contrast, Mexico and the Caribbean, an area totaling only about five and a half million acres, or about one-eighth as much land, provides wintering habitat for nearly half of these neotropical migrant species. Clearing an acre in Mexico then, may be equivalent in its effect on birds to destroying eight or ten acres on Long Island.

The effects of fragmentation can be severe as well. A number of studies, some quite ingenious in design, have demonstrated that neotropical migrants such as the wood thrush and ovenbird have less reproductive success in small woodlots than they do in larger unbroken forest tracts, due to the creation of "edge" habitat (the meeting ground between different habitat types). Many predators such as fox, raccoon, and opossum frequent edge habitats, since food sources tend to be more abundant.

The brown-headed cowbird, a nest parasite that lays its eggs in the nests of other birds, has had a significant impact on many neotropical migrants, parasitizing as much as seventy-five percent of the nests of some species in certain areas. Brown-headed cowbirds also frequent edge habitat and are known to penetrate several hundred yards into forested lots in their search for nests. This means that lots of less than an acre, a few acres, or in some cases dozens of acres are functionally serving as edge habitat.

Given these findings ecologists have promoted the concepts of preserving large unbroken tracts of land, preferably with a square or round configuration, since these shapes have lower perimeter-to-area ratios; acquiring corridors to link heretofore unconnected properties; and in parks where facilities are planned, placing the ballfield or parking lot on the periphery of the property, leaving the heart of the tract intact.

If we are to protect migrant songbirds, preserving large tracts of contiguous land seems to be the key.

Where To See Songbirds

During the peak of spring migration songbirds can be found in just about any suitable habitat of any size, ranging from the half dozen oak trees in your backyard to a state park, thousands of acres in size. As a general rule of thumb, songbird migration is heavier in the western portion of the Island. Songbirds avoid flying over water if they can. They stay along the coast and fan out into New England once they pass New York City, instead of breaking across the New York Bight and Long Island Sound into New England.

Forest Park in Queens and **Prospect Park** and the **Greenwood Cemetery** in Brooklyn are reliable places to enjoy spring migration, as are the gardens at **Jamaica Bay Refuge** (on the west side of Cross Bay Boulevard). **Valley Stream** and **Hempstead State Parks** can be productive as well. Several places at **Jones Beach State Park** are worth visiting including the area around Zach's Bay and the Hedge Row immediately south of the Coast Guard Station near the west end. Also, the parks in the Nassau County park system and the county parks in the western part of Suffolk County are likely to provide an enjoyable birding experience. Outside the range of this book is **Central Park** in Manhattan, but it is worth mentioning since it has acted as a magnet for birds and birders for many years. The area of The Ramble, situated between the lake and the East 79th Street/West 81st Street cross-through, can be particularly productive.

Key Times

Approximately — April 20th to May 25th.
Early morning and late afternoon are the times of day migrating songbirds are most active.

Bluebirds in rapture,
tumble from a perch of oak —
the sky is falling.

EPICORMIC BRANCHING ON PITCH PINE. (Robert T. McGrath)

CHAPTER NINE

Lick of Flame

FIRE IN THE LONG ISLAND FOREST

Many factors play a role in shaping the structure and character of a natural community. From a regional perspective, climate is a significant influence, and from a local point of view, soil type, topography, specific weather-related events, human disturbance and other factors can play important roles.

Although we classify wildfire under "other factors," its effect on Long Island's natural communities is telling. There are probably only a couple of places on the Island that have never burned, and conversely, there are several communities, including the Hempstead Plains, Oak Brush Plains, Dwarf Pine Plains and maritime grasslands, that either depend on, or are strongly influenced by, wildfire. The jack pine forests of Michigan, the sawgrass wetlands of Florida's Everglades and the chaparral in California are three other communities out of several dozen occurring throughout the country which are shaped by fire.

As you might expect, plants and animals living in these fire-prone areas exhibit a remarkable spectrum of adaptations to wildfire. Pitch pine, the dominant pine of the Pine Barrens, for example, has very thick bark which chars, but rarely burns, thereby insulating the growing cambium layer beneath. Also, mature trees display a phenomenon called *epicormic* (meaning upon the skin) *branching*, where dormant buds between the bark plates begin to elongate in response to fire, eventually forming new branches to replace those consumed in the fire.

When fire kills the above-ground portion of younger pitch pines, from sapling size to about ten feet tall, one or more basal crook buds will begin to grow. Situated at the soil surface and on the underside of the S-shaped crook or bend in the young pine, the buds elongate into shoots. Eventually one of the shoots becomes dominant and forms the new trunk. In these examples, the black-colored charcoal of the burnt trunks and branches provides a somber backdrop to the bright, lime-green shoots of the recovering pine. Perhaps the most remarkable adaptation is displayed by the closed cones found on dwarf pitch pines (for more details, see sidebar article on Dwarf Pine Plains in Chapter 21).

Other plants, such as scrub and dwarf chestnut oak, black huckleberry and various blueberries, demonstrate a remarkable ability to recover from regular fire. In fact, the abundance of these plant species is a strong indication of regularly occurring fires. Tree-sized oaks, such as black, scarlet, white and red, while not able to recover from a series of intense burns occurring at short intervals, can survive a fire schedule that involves fire once every decade or so. Armed with the knowledge of a plant's response to a particular fire regime (a natural fire frequency), you can look at a community and make some educated guesses about the role of fire in it. For example, in the Pine Barrens, it is known that areas that have more pitch pine and less oak in the tree canopy burn more frequently, and that the converse is true: areas where tree oaks dominate probably have less intense, less frequent burns. Taking it a step further, areas that are dominated by the dwarf oak species have a greater fire frequency than those dominated by pine, and a grassland which can tolerate annual burns (e.g. the Hempstead Plains) will take hold over a dwarf oak area if fires are frequent enough.

In contrast, along roadsides or at the edge of housing developments in the Pine Barrens, you are likely to find plants such as sassafras, hickory and green brier which are clear indications of a fire-suppressed environment. The public is beginning to recognize, albeit slowly, that fire is a factor which has influenced the character of natural communities throughout the United States, as well as here on Long Island. Lagging behind this recognition though, is the next logical step: actively restoring the role of wildfire in shaping the character of the Island's vegetation, and discontinuing the practice of complete fire suppression. Currently, fire departments on Long Island snuff out of virtually all woodland wildfires.

One thing we know is that these communities, given their predisposition to burn (aided by the sandy, porous soils which easily drain moisture from the surface), are going to continue to burn whether the fires are promptly put out or not. Therefore, a policy of fire suppression and extinguishment fails on two counts: it does not serve to protect the public from a major conflagration that is a likely result of continuously increasing fuel loads, and it does not allow fire to play its traditional role of maintaining the distinctive character of these fire climax forests.

This reactive policy of fire suppression should be replaced by a proactive policy, where appropriate public land agencies initiate controlled or prescribed burns. A prescribed burn is one that is planned, based on a window of environmental conditions, and designed to accomplish certain ecological or public safety objectives. If a comprehensive, scientifically rigorous prescribed burn program were implemented, not only could the unique natural character of a community be perpetuated, but the likelihood of an out-of-control fire, with all its tragic consequences to human health and property, would be reduced.

The Nature Conservancy has conducted controlled burns on many of its preserves for ecological reasons, and many state forest service agencies intentionally set their forest lands on fire to reduce fuel loads. Indeed, the Long Island Chapter of The Nature Conservancy has begun to develop a prescribed burn program and has conducted several small burns, most notably at the nineteen-acre Hempstead Plains Preserve in Uniondale.

Where To See The Influence Of Fire On Long Island

Numerous fires of various sizes occur annually on Long Island, so there is no shortage of places to visit to see the effects of fire on vegetation. An interesting project involves finding a tract of woodland that has recently burned and monitoring its recovery over the span of several years.

Connetquot River State Park — Despite the policy of extreme fire suppression practiced by park personnel, exemplified by the number and extent of fire breaks dissecting the property, the park is a mosaic of fire-influenced communities. Some sections have burned recently, others not for several years, and still others not in many years.

New York State Edgewood Oak Brush Plains Preserve — this preserve, like Connetquot, contains a mosaic of community types, but being about one-sixth the size, the property can be covered in a morning hike.

Along the Long Island Expressway — Northwestern corner of Exit 66: the property on the west side of County Route 21, and on the north side of the westbound service road, burned in the spring of 1990 and is currently recovering. Also: the south side of the Expressway about 1/2 mile east of Exit 68; and the north side of the Expressway about 1/2 mile east of Exit 70.

Brookhaven State Park — in the south end of the state park (in Ridge) bordering Route 25, across from East Margin Drive. This burn, occurred about eight years ago, and was so intense that it killed many tree-sized pitch pine.

CHAPTER TEN

BIRD'S FOOT VIOLET. (Robert T. McGrath)

Long Island's Prairie

THE HEMPSTEAD PLAINS

It may be a difficult task, particularly if you know from firsthand experience the extent to which central Nassau County has been built up, but try to imagine standing in the vicinity of the Veterans Memorial Coliseum in Uniondale, waist high in grasses and wildflowers. Your view is an unbroken, 360-degree sweep to the horizon with nothing but prairie in sight. This experience, while impossible today, was probably available to your parents and certainly to your grandparents.

The Hempstead Plains, by which this community is known, once encompassed tens of thousands of acres (estimates run from 17,000 to 60,000 acres) across the center of Nassau County. Its western border began in the vicinity of Floral Park and continued eastward, melding into the Pine Barrens communities of the Oak Brush Plains, near the modern-day Nassau/Suffolk county line. To the north it was bordered by hardwood forests covering the Ronkonkoma Moraine, and to the south by a belt of oak that extended to the bay.

Daniel Denton knew of the Hempstead Plains, reporting, "Toward the middle of Long Island lyeth a plain, sixteen miles long and four broad, upon which plain grows very fine grass that makes excellent good hay, and is very good pasture for sheep and other cattle; where you shall find neither stick nor stone to hinder the horseheels or endanger them in their races."

More than 145 species of grasses, wildflowers and shrubs have been recorded from the Plains, providing a field day for the botanically inclined. Birds-foot violet, one of the more well-known species, reportedly bloomed in such profusion that in the spring, before the emergence of the prairie grasses, it painted a pale purple haze. Photographs still exist of visitors carried out into the Plains by horse and buggy to pick the flowers for Easter bouquets.

Other wildflowers include wild indigo, American goat's-rue, blue toadflax, dogbane, colicroot, cinquefoils, various milkweeds and goldenrods. Most recently, sandplain gerardia, perhaps the rarest wildflower in the northeastern United States, and known from only a handful of locations worldwide, was discovered in a remnant tract of the Hempstead Plains.

Several grassland bird species once occurred, including the upland sandpiper, grasshopper and vesper sparrows and horned larks.

It is the grasses, however, that predominate. Several species occur here which impart a prairielike effect, including little and big bluestem, Indian grass and several species of bent and panic grasses.

A definitive explanation of the factor or factors that created the Hempstead Plains has not yet been discovered and may never be, due to the extent of its destruction. Based on the influences which have shaped prairies in the midwest, though, it is reasonable to assume its cause was at least partly due to interrelated influences: regular wildfires; the development of a dense, interwoven organic mat referred to as "prairie sod;" droughty, porous soils and subsoils; and, during colonial times, the effects of grazing livestock.

The open, treeless nature of the area, combined with its flat topography, made the Plains ideal for farming and later, during the late 1940s, for home construction. By the late 1960s, the little bit that remained of the Plains fell within Mitchell Field, which was then county owned. Tragically, despite the fact that ninety-five percent of the Plains had been destroyed, the Nassau County government had no interest in establishing a meaningful preserve with the hundreds of acres that it owned.

Where To See The Hempstead Plains

Today, less than one hundred acres remain of this once vast and unique wonder: two preserves of sixty and nineteen acres, and the rough areas surrounding the public golf courses at Eisenhower Park, which are reverting to prairie vegetation now that the County Parks Department has eliminated mowing. The best example of the three is the nineteen-acre parcel situated east of Nassau Community College and north of Charles Lindbergh Boulevard, adjacent to the student commuter parking lot. The property, owned by the College and co-managed with the Long Island Chapter of The Nature Conservancy, is fenced and gated. To learn the combination of the gate lock and of activity restrictions, call the Long Island Chapter at (516) 367-3225.

Key Times

While each season provides a reason to visit the Hempstead Plains, the profusion of blossoming wildflowers during spring and summer probably make them the best seasons to visit. During the fall, when the prairie grasses have turned various shades of russet and gold, is also a nice time to visit the Plains.

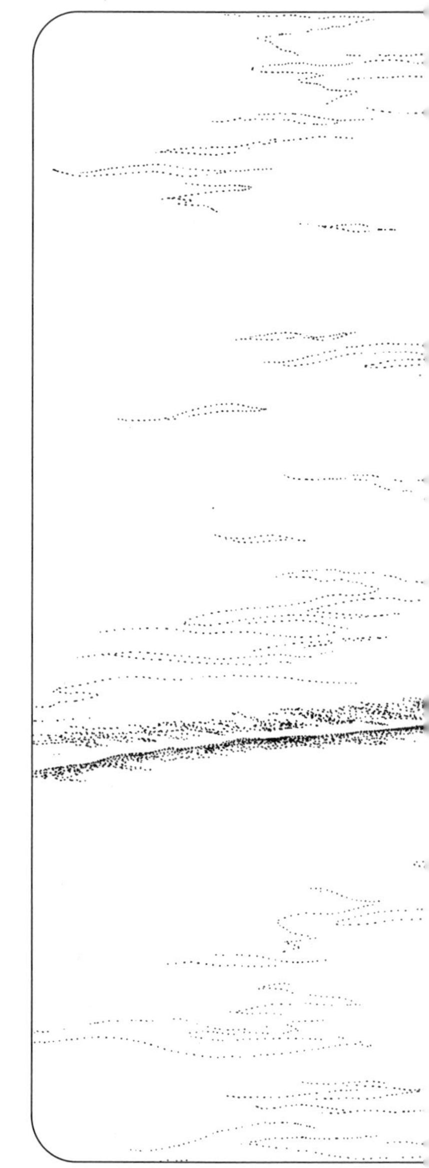

BLACK SKIMMER. (Maria T. Weisenberg)

Summer

PRICKLY PEAR CACTUS. (Robert T. McGrath)

CHAPTER ELEVEN

The Prickly Pear

LONG ISLAND'S NATIVE CACTUS

You are hiking with some friends along a trail that runs through an area cloaked with beach grass. You notice the plants: a clump of dusty miller on one side of the path and a patch of beach clotbur on the other. A few feet ahead, another plant catches your eye. If you did not know better, you would swear it was a type of cactus. Not sure though, you mutter underneath your breath to your friends, "I didn't know any cactus was found on Long Island."

But it is. You are not seeing things. The prickly pear cactus, *Opuntia humifusa*, is a native wildflower and Long Island's sole representative of the desert-adapted family. It is one of the most spectacular flowering plants found here.

Each plant produces at least one, but often two or more flowers, positioned on top of the cactus. They are showy, bright yellow and are up to three to four inches wide. The stamens and pistil (the male and female parts of the flower respectively) are quite conspicuous. The flowers bloom from late June through mid-July.

The pads of the plant are reminiscent of the sole of a shoe; some are straight, others curved. They are covered with conspicuous, one-inch-long spines growing in groups of three. Not so conspicuous are the scores of minute bristles that cover the pads. These can be very irritating if imbedded in flesh. Therefore, you are strongly advised not to touch the plant barehanded.

The fruits of the cactus are about an inch long and three-quarters of an inch wide. They are green at first, but turn a pretty maroon as they mature Inside, their pulp is bright purple and quite edible (hence their other common name, Indian fig). They have become popular items in gourmet food stores. The fruits do not have bristles, but the caution noted above still applies. The seeds are large and woody.

Prickly pear often grows in dense colonies consisting of hundreds of plants, and in any colony a number of different growth forms can be seen. Some are straight and upright reaching a height of about eighteen inches, while others trail along the ground. The species name, *humifusa*, means "to trail" in Latin, and the generic name, *Opuntia*, comes from the name of a town in ancient Greece. Perhaps a plant that resembled prickly pear cactus grew near this town.

Not only is the prickly pear the only cactus native to Long Island, it is the only cactus found in the eastern United States. This is surprising since there are more than two hundred species of prickly pear found in the western hemisphere, of which dozens occur in the western United States. Yet only *humifusa* has been able to colonize the eastern United States. Why this is so remains one of the unsolved puzzles of plant geography.

On Long Island, the cactus prefers dry, sandy soils. As a result, it commonly grows in heavily vegetated habitats adjacent to beaches.

Where To See Prickly Pear Cactus

Prickly pear occurs in dozens of locations throughout the Island. The following sites contain some of the larger colonies.

Indian Island County Park — Riverhead. A large population of cactus is found immediately to the south of the public campground adjacent to Saw Mill Creek.

Orient Point State Park — Southold. A colony of cactus is growing adjacent to the main pavilion.

Caumsett State Park — Lloyd Neck. A colony is growing along the upper beach in the northwestern section of the park.

West Meadow Beach and **Flax Pond** — Old Field. Hundreds of plants are found on the east side of the road at West Meadow Beach, and a smaller concentration occurs along the beach in the northwestern corner of the Flax Pond property managed by the New York State Department of Environmental Conservation.

Nissequogue Nature Preserve — Smithtown. A colony is situated adjacent to the parking lot.

Sammy's Beach — East Hampton. A spread-out population is found along the front lawns of the summer homes that make up this vacation community, situated on the west side of Three Mile Harbor.

Key Times

Flowers — Late June through mid-July

Fruits — September through early November

ARETHUSA ORCHID. (Robert T. McGrath)

CHAPTER TWELVE

Orchids

VARIATIONS ON A THEME

There probably is no other group of plants that has generated as much horticultural, botanical and ecological interest as members of the family *Orchidaceae*, the orchids. While primarily a family of the tropics, where nearly 20,000 species flourish (many in the treetops), some orchids are found as far north as the arctic treeline.

A total of thirty-five species have been recorded from Long Island, although not that many exist here today, due to extirpation. While there is uncertainty as to the number of species remaining, at least two dozen orchids still occur. They range from species represented by one small population to those that are widespread and common.

The **pink lady's slipper,** or Indian moccasin, is the best known native orchid. Growing in dry to mixed woodlands, such as oak/pitch pine forests, this showy wildflower has two inconspicuous lateral petals to each side and a prominent, deep-pink lip petal that forms a conspicuous frontal pouch. The shape of the lip petal acts quite successfully in dispersing pollen. An insect, escaping the pouch after a search for nectar, rubs against a waxy patch of pollen known as a pollinia. Easily detached, this sticky patch of pollen accompanies the insect to the next lady's slipper where some of the pollen can fertilize the flower.

The lady's slipper illustrates a basic pattern in orchid flower architecture: the three petals are arranged so that the two side petals are dominated by a conspicuous lip petal, prominent due to its color, size or fine dissection. The three sepals are inconspicuous. Recognizing this similarity in anatomy, it is interesting to compare the "variations on a theme" displayed by our native orchids.

The lady's slipper flower rises on a slender stalk between two arching, prominently veined, basal leaves. It can take more than a dozen years for a lady's slipper to become sexually mature and to send up a flower. Immature plants, often outnumbering the mature plants at a site, are represented by single arching leaves.

Rose pogonia, the essence of which has been beautifully captured by Robert Frost's poem "Rose Pogonias," is rose pink in color (rarely white) and inhabits open wetland areas. It is especially common in former cranberry bogs. Its slender flower stalk, displaying a single oval leaf at the midway point, rises eight to ten inches above a thicket of cranberry vines, rushes and sedges. Because of its ability to propagate vegetatively (by the use of underground runners or rhizomes), rose pogonia can form extensive colonies containing hundreds of plants.

Rose pogonia is also known as snakemouth, due to the similarity of the brightly colored, fringed lip petal to the mouth of a serpent. The species name, *ophioglossoides*, is Greek for "like a snake's tongue."

Snakemouth should not be confused with dragon's-mouth, an alternative name for the **arethusa orchid,** which is an uncommon cousin of the rose pogonia. The dragon's-mouth grows in sandy, boglike environs, often in association with sphagnum moss. Its flower is similar to the snakemouth's, except that the lip petal tends to arch more (like the tongue of a sick patient during a doctor's examination). The petal is also wider and has purple spots.

Calopogon, or grass-pink (because of its grasslike leaf), grows in some of the same bog habitats as the rose pogonia. It is easily distinguished from the latter by its deeper, magenta-colored flowers which, unlike the pogonia or arethusa which produce single flowers, are usually found in pairs (sometimes threes). Perhaps its most distinctive feature is that the lip petal is at the top, as if some boggy sylvan took a pogonia flower and turned it 180 degrees. The lip is fringed and brightly colored.

Several species of **fringed orchids** occur on the Island, including the white-fringed, yellow-fringed, purple-fringed, crested-fringed (or crested-yellow as it is sometimes called), ragged-fringed and northern wood orchis. These orchids get their common name from the highly dissected or fringed lip petal which gives a lacy, fragile look to the flowers. They are also known as the "rein" orchids because of the long spur, or rein, that trails at the end of the flower.

The white-fringed has a preference for sandy waterlogged soils along the edges of bogs or in wet meadows. The yellow-fringed is found growing along roadsides and other disturbed habitats, while the crested-yellow is found in pine barrens areas with few understory plants. Ragged-fringed is found in a variety of habitats, but seems to be most common in old fields and other open habitats. The purple-fringed and wood orchis prefer damp, mature woodland.

Another distinctive group of orchids are the **rattlesnake-plantains,** so named because of the resemblance of the highly reticulated (checkered white and green) basal leaves to the skin of a rattlesnake. Originally three species were native to the Island, but today only the downy rattlesnake plantain remains. It grows in dry to moist woods, and the two dozen or so flowers grow in a spike that may reach a foot and a half high.

The **ladies' tresses** are represented by four species. Named because of the resemblance of the flowers to the tresses worn by the ladies of yesteryear, these distinctive orchids grow in fields, along roads and in other disturbed habitats. The flowers are twisted in a spiral around the stem, a growth form suggested by their generic name, *Spiranthes*.

The **whorled pogonia** (no close relation to the rose pogonia) is a woodland orchid that has a greenish-yellow flower with a three-lobed lip petal. The flower is framed by sepals that are two to three times longer than it, giving the flower a tropical look. A whorl of five leaves (hence the common name) occurs at the top of the stem. The whorled pogonia is found in both dry and rich woodlands.

A smaller cousin to the whorled pogonia, commonly called the **small whorled pogonia,** historically has been documented as occurring on Long Island, but has not been seen by anyone in decades. Listed and protected as a federally endangered species, it is one of the rarest wildflowers in the eastern United States. If you wish to become famous in botanical circles and be feted at naturalist dinners, be the first one to locate a population of this plant on Long Island.

The **cranefly orchid** is one of the rarer orchids known to exist on Long Island. One population of several dozen plants occurs in a rich woodland on the North Fork. It was named the cranefly orchid due to the fact the slender flowers look like so many craneflies suspended in space.

The flower stalk emerges in early August and is replaced in the fall by a single purple-green-colored leaf.

Where To See Orchids

Almost all native orchids have declined, some alarmingly so. While this decline is primarily due to habitat destruction, indiscriminate picking and digging of these highly prized wildflowers has been a contributing factor. Digging orchids to sell or transplant is a futile exercise since plants invariably die. Orchids depend upon specific soil fungi in order to survive, and the fungi are easily destroyed when the plants are dug up. As a result, specific sites where these species occur are not listed. Instead, you are encouraged to participate in scheduled field trips sponsored by organizations such as the Long Island Botanical Society.

Key Times

Pink lady's slipper — May
Rose pogonia, arethusa, calopogon — June
Whorled pogonia — late June
Rattlesnake plantain — July
Fringed orchids — early August
Cranefly orchid — early August
Ladies' tresses — mid-August

CHAPTER THIRTEEN

INDIAN PIPE. (Robert T. McGrath)

Dead Man's Fingers

AND OTHER PARASITES

If awards were given to the plant with the most imaginative name, the sure winner would be **Indian pipe,** *Monotropa uniflora*. Not only has it been named after a smoking instrument used by Native Americans (the plant does look like a pipe, but it certainly was not used to inhale anything), it has also been called convulsion weed, due to its apparent emetic properties, and ice plant, based on the icy look of the translucent flower and stem. But the best (and certainly most macabre) names refer to the plant's white, waxy stem and flower head: dead man's fingers, ghost flower and corpse plant. While perhaps a bit gruesome to envision, a bunch of stalks can resemble the upright hand of a dead person, partially buried in the leaves. Scarier still, it could be the hand of an emerging monster from one of those horror flicks that always seem to be popular.

The derivation of the Latin name seems tame by comparison. *Monotropa* means "one turn" in Greek, a reference to the nodding flower head which turns upward once it is pollinated. (It also turns black and dries out.) *Uniflora* means "one flower" referring to the fact that each flowering stalk is topped by a single flower. Once the flowers are pollinated they transform into woody capsules that split sideways, releasing the seeds contained within.

Indian pipe is a perennial plant, meaning that it emerges from one year to the next in the same location from the same rootstock. Its "leaves" are restricted to small scales that hug the stem. Emerging from the ground in bunches with as few as two to as many as twelve plants, Indian pipe stands out with its white stalk and flower (occasionally light pink) contrasted against the dark brown leaf litter. The plant is translucent white because it lacks chlorophyll and therefore is unable to photosynthesize its own food. It derives the energy it needs by adopting a parasitic way of life: it taps into the hyphae of intertwined soil fungi, obtaining nutrients stored therein. The fungi are also parasitic and tap into green plants in order to capture the nutritional benefits of photosynthesis.

Indian pipe is not the only Long Island wildflower to evolve a parasitic lifestyle. **Pinesap,** a close relative of the Indian pipe, is distinguished by its multi-flowered and colored stalk (running from tan to a rust-red). It is a parasitic plant in both oak and pine forests. **Beechdrops,** a member of the broomrape family which contains a host of parasitic brethren, taps into the roots of beech trees. Its generic name, *Epifagus*, literally means "upon the beech." The plant is colored tan with several thin stems, each of which have ten to twenty small, tan and purple-streaked flowers. They can sometimes be found by the hundreds, flowering beneath majestic American beech trees. A close relative of beechdrops, **squawroot,** has a dense flower head containing dozens of flowers each; it is parasitic on tree roots, with a preference for oaks.

Where To See Parasitic Plants

Indian pipe is the most widespread of the species mentioned. It can be found fairly easily in dry oak forests, pine groves and occasionally in very dense cover. (Since the plant does not need to photosynthesize, it can tolerate low light conditions.) It can be seen in **Forest, Cunningham** and **Alley Pond Parks** in Queens, **Massapequa State Preserve, Connetquot River State Park Preserve, Caleb Smith State Park Preserve,** and **West Hills, Blydenburgh, Southaven, Cathedral** and **Prosser Pines County Parks.**

Pinesap has a more restricted range, but is known from the Walking Dunes area of **Hither Hills State Park** and is common growing beneath pitch pine in **Napeague State Park.** It also can be found at **Caumsett State Park** and **Robert C. Murphy** and **West Hills County Parks.**

Beechdrops, not surprisingly, only occur where there are beech trees. It is common in the western section of **Alley Pond Park** and can be seen at **Montauk County Park** in the rich woods situated south of **Big Reed Pond.** Also, it occurs in the eastern section of the **David Weld Preserve,** located in Nissequogue and managed by the Long Island Chapter of The Nature Conservancy.

Squawroot occurs at the **Shu Swamp Preserve** in Mill Neck.

Key Times

Indian pipe and **pinesap** — early July through early August

Beechdrops — August through early September

Squawroot — Late May through early June

BLUE LUPINE. (Robert T. McGrath)

CHAPTER FOURTEEN

"Please Pass the Peas"

Observing and identifying native wildflowers is one of the pleasures of nature study, and many enthusiasts find members of the pea or legume family particularly interesting. A reason seems to be that there are so many cousins to the well-known garden pea growing wild in Long Island's fields and forests. These wildflowers can be segregated into five major groups: blue lupine, American goat's-rue, wild indigo, the bush clovers and tick trefoils.

Leguminous wildflowers share certain characteristics. They have compound leaves, or leaves that are divided into smaller leaflets (compared to entire leaves which have just one continuous leaf surface, such as an oak or maple leaf). Their flowers, though of various sizes and colors, are similar to that of the garden pea, most having five petals. The two side petals are called wings, the two lower petals, keels, and the upper petal is known as the banner.

Blue lupine is one of the more distinctive examples of the group. It has palmately compound leaves, meaning the leaflets radiate from a central point as the fingers do from the palm of a hand. In the case of the lupine, seven to eleven "fingers" is the norm. It grows in sandy soils and has flowers ranging in color from pale to dark violet. Lupine is common in several locations within the Pine Barrens, with local populations ranging from single plants to colonies of hundreds of plants.

The scientific name for blue lupine is *Lupinus perennis*. The species name, *perennis*, refers to the perennial nature of the plant, while the generic name, *Lupinus*, is derived from the Latin name for the wolf: *lupus*. Some imaginative naturalist likened the wolf's ability to steal sheep to the ability of this robust plant to "steal" its food from the sandy, nutrient-poor soil in which it grows. As we now know, all legumes are able to fix nitrogen from the air into the soil surrounding their roots, thereby augmenting the nutrients available to the plant and enriching the soil.

American goat's rue also has compound leaves, but in its case they are known as pinnately compound leaves, a reference to the leaflets being arranged on the leaf like the pinnae of a bird's feather. It has distinctive tri-colored flowers of yellow, raspberry and purple that are bunched at the top of the plant. The plant stem takes on a grayish or silvery appearance due to the presence of hundreds of tiny, downy hairs (which is the derivation of its generic name, *Tephrosia*). Scattered plants grow along sandy trails and roads, particularly in the Pine Barrens.

Wild indigo grows in the same habitats as goat's rue. Its flowers are bright yellow and are scattered at the end of sprawling leaves. During the growing season the stem of the plant is dark blue, and if it is broken, a dye or tincture of that color will exude. That is the source of the plant's species name, *tinctoria*. This dye was one of the few sources of the color blue available to Native Americans.

Both the **bush clovers** and **tick trefoils** have small flowers. (The latter plant was so named because of the compound leaves of three leaflets each and the similarity in appearance of the seed pods to ticks.) In the bush clovers the flowers form a dense head of dozens of flowers atop the plant, while the tick trefoil flowers are fewer and scattered at the end of the branches in a pattern similar to wild indigo. There are more than ten species of these two interesting groups native to Long Island.

A number of other pea species have been introduced to Long Island and are now common. These plants include a tree, the black locust, with its blossoms of fragrant, creamy-white flowers hanging in pendulous droops. Others are the vinelike vetches, several sweet clovers, bird's-foot trefoil, everlasting pea and, of course, the ubiquitous red, white and rabbit-foot clovers found in many a lawn and school yard.

Where To See Peas

The members of the pea family discussed above are widespread throughout Long Island in dry, sandy environments. Blue Lupine is common along North Street in Manorville; a small population is found on the northeast corner of County Route 111 and Halsey Manor Road; and several dozen plants are situated on the road shoulder of State Route 27 at the point it narrows from two lanes to one about one and a half miles east of the Shinnecock Canal Bridge. It is also common along many roads that traverse the middle of the South Fork.

WILD INDIGO, GOAT'S RUE, THE BUSH CLOVERS and **TICK TREFOILS** are most common in the **Pine Barrens** and can be found along trails and in openings in virtually all parks containing pine barrens vegetation, including: **Connetquot River State Park Preserve, Edgewood State Preserve, Brookhaven State Park, Robert C. Murphy County Park,** the Department of Environmental Conservation's **Rocky Point** and **Riverhead Properties** and the **Dwarf Pine Plains.**

Key Times

LUPINE, WILD INDIGO, and **GOAT'S RUE** bloom from late spring through early summer. The bush clovers and tick trefoils flower in mid- to late summer.

CHAPTER FIFTEEN

SWEET BAY MAGNOLIA. (Robert T. McGrath)

The Atlantic White Cedar and Sweet Bay Magnolia

At one time, both the Atlantic white cedar and the sweet bay magnolia were fairly common on Long Island. Inhabiting forested, freshwater wetlands, they were widespread in suitable locations throughout the western part of the Island, particularly along streams that dissected the south shore. The community of Cedarhurst is believed to have been named in recognition of a large white cedar swamp that once occurred in the area.

Both trees have been victims of development, and have been substantially reduced, due to the filling and draining of wetland habitats and to systematic overharvesting.

Atlantic white cedar, also called the coast, swamp, post and southern cedar, is found from Maine to Florida. The tree has a restricted range along the Atlantic and Gulf coasts and never strays far from them. The most inland stands of cedar known are in North Carolina, about 115 miles from the coast. The most abundant stands are found in the famous Dismal Swamp, straddling the Virginia-North Carolina border. In New York all remaining populations of the cedar, except one, are located on Long Island.

As the wood is light, strong and highly resistant to insect and fungal attack, the tree was once in great demand for shingling, boat-building, fence posts and utility poles. It was also one of the first woods used in making pipe organs.

White cedar has a number of distinctive characteristics. Its foliage is an attractive dark green. The leaves of the tree are minute and scale-like, no more than one-fifth of an inch in length. The top side of the leaf is dotted with resinous glands, and the bottom has a little keel. Leaves on young plants and on the leading shoots of grown trees are prickly and bristlelike.

The branches are slender and droopy with ends flaring into fan-shaped sprays. The bark is fairly smooth, thin (rarely more than half an inch) and often peels away from the trunk in fibrous strips, providing prime nesting material for a variety of birds. On older trees the bark is invariably spiraled a half turn, as if Paul Bunyan had firmly grasped the top and bottom of the tree and twisted.

The columnar trunks are arrow-straight (hence their use in ship-building and utility poles) and can reach seventy to ninety feet in height, with a diameter of one to four feet. Individuals have been found that are more than 1,000 years old, but on Long Island there are only a few specimens that are more than fifty feet tall and 100 years old.

You might expect a tree that reaches such dimensions to have large pine cones, maybe a foot long as in the longleaf pine, or at least several inches as in the pitch pine. If so, you will be disappointed to learn that the cones of the white cedar are pea-sized. Immature cones are green with a blue-white bloom. They turn a pretty blue-purple as they mature, and finally become reddish brown and woody.

The average cone produces ten tiny seeds. A patient dendrologist, writing in a 1931 United States Forest Service monograph on the species, determined that it takes between 420,000 and 500,000 seeds to make up a pound! The seeds are double-winged to facilitate dispersal and can travel as far as a mile in a strong wind, thereby allowing the species to colonize new sites.

Atlantic white cedar is restricted to wetland environments, showing a preference for the acidic, organic, waterlogged soils of peat bogs. It has a fairly narrow tolerance to water levels, though, and cannot survive in soils that are either totally saturated or too dry. Small depressions are ideal for the establishment of a stand of white cedar. Being low, they collect water which attracts other wetland plants. As these plants decompose, they generate the bed of peat that cedars prefer. A grove of several acres in North Sea (on the north side of the South Fork) has peat that has been measured to a depth of nineteen feet.

Living in peat, however, has its hazards. During droughts, water table levels drop, allowing the peat to dry. If a wildfire ensues, it can burn most or all of the highly flammable peat, killing the thin-barked cedars. This leads to a high probability that all cedars will die at the same time, and is the reason one finds many uniform stands of even-aged cedars. The young, germinated from seeds that survive in the peat, grow quickly in the open, sunlit habitat that was formerly, and soon will be again, a cedar swamp.

Atlantic white cedar should not be confused with two of its cousins. Northern white cedar (also known as arborvitae) is not native to Long Island, although an ornamental variety of the species is widely planted. It ranges in suitable wetland sites throughout the northeastern United States and eastern Canada. Red cedar, actually a juniper, is abundant on Long Island growing in a variety of upland situations, including old fields and coastal habitats, where it often is the first tree to become established.

Sweet bay magnolia has little in common with Atlantic white cedar, other than that it too is a wetland plant. While white cedar can reach scores of feet into the sky, sweet bay magnolia, at least in the northern part of its range, rarely exceeds twenty feet and is mostly an understory plant in the swamps in which it grows. Due to its diminutive stature, the wood has little commercial value, and for the most part it escaped the saw. However, it was harvested in significant numbers by nurserymen who prized its showy, white flowers.

Sweet bay magnolia has a broader range than the white cedar and is found throughout the southeastern United States. Its flowers, creamy-white, wonderfully fragrant and two to three inches in diameter, are as conspicuous as the cedar's cones are unobtrusive. And while the leaves of cedar are small, magnolia leaves are three to five inches long and two inches wide.

Cedars in the Sea

Long Island is losing its battle with the sea, and nowhere is this more evident than at Montauk Point. The many fallen boulders scattered on the beach are a clear indication of the erosive force of the ocean. But there is a subtle, more interesting sign: white cedar stumps imbedded in the ocean bottom.

These remnants, visible at low tide along the north side of the State Park near the concession building, were undoubtedly once part of a cedar stand that stood several hundred yards from the shoreline. The resistant nature of cedar wood has no doubt enabled these stumps to survive.

Where To See Atlantic White Cedar and Sweet Bay Magnolia

There are approximately thirty separate stands of Atlantic white cedar remaining on Long Island. They range from just a few trees to groves several acres in size. IT IS IMPORTANT TO WALK CAREFULLY IN A CEDAR SWAMP because seedling trees, only a few inches tall, are hard to see and can be easily trampled. It is best to view a cedar grove from its edge.

For **WHITE CEDAR:**

Sears-Bellows County Park — Flanders. This park has the most extensive stands of cedar remaining on Long Island. White cedar occurs along the edges of most of the ponds; a grove of what may be a unique population of dwarf cedars occurs at Division Pond.

Owl Pond/Birch Creek County Park — Flanders.

Hubbard County Park — Flanders

Cranberry Bog County Nature Preserve — Riverside. Stands occur throughout the park. Look for them along the edge of Swezey's and Cedar Ponds.

Tackapausha County Nature Preserve — Seaford. The grove is situated in the southeastern corner of the preserve and is best viewed from the bridge that crosses the stream near Seaford Avenue.

Quogue Wildlife Refuge — Quogue, throughout the refuge.

Blydenburgh County Park — Hauppauge. A grove is in the southwestern corner of park; another smaller grove is located in a pond on the south side of Veteran's Memorial Highway about 100 yards west of the County Park entrance.

Only one population of **SWEET BAY MAGNOLIA** remains on Long Island. It is situated in a swamp on the west side of the **Speonk River** north of Montauk Highway in Speonk.

Key Times

SWEET BAY MAGNOLIA — Flowers bloom in mid to late June.
ATLANTIC WHITE CEDAR — Anytime of year; cones form in the fall.

Along a roadway,
young cedar in fence shadow,
avoids the mowing.

THREAD-LEAVED SUNDEW. (Robert T. McGrath)

CHAPTER SIXTEEN

Plants that Eat Animals

Certainly you have seen low budget sci-fi thrillers where a huge plant runs amok, eating people and other animals in its path, before it is brought under control in the end by the movie's hero and heroine. While movie producers have exaggerated the ability of plants to eat animals, the principle is based on fact, and we have nearly a dozen plants on Long Island to prove it.

But you can relax; neither you nor your pet is likely to become a statistic. The overwhelming source of animal protein for these plants is derived from insects and other small invertebrates.

The three groups of plants — pitcher plants, sundews and bladderworts — have devised very different means for capturing their animal prey. The **pitcher plant,** which has several features that make it a highly effective killing machine, is a wetland-loving plant that belongs to a family common to the southeastern United States (where its close cousin, the trumpets, occur). On Long Island it grows primarily in the acid bogs of the Pine Barrens which are dominated by sphagnum moss and leatherleaf.

The plant's name refers to the distinctive eight-inch, pitcher-shaped leaves which collect rainwater. Near the top of the pitcher, at the point where it constricts, is a ring of sticky, easily dislodged cells. Insects losing their footing in this zone, slip into the next zone dominated by thousands of minute, downward-pointing hairs. These hairs make it very difficult for insects that have flown or fallen in to walk back up the pitcher to freedom. After struggling for awhile, the hapless insect falls into the water and eventually drowns. The plant then exudes digestive juices from special cells in its leaves and digests the inner, soft parts of its prey. The chitinous exoskeleton, all that is left, sinks to the bottom of the pitcher.

Blooming in late June or early July, the flower of the pitcher plant is as distinctive as the leaves. Usually produced singly, it is large (two inches across), burgundy in color and grows on a stalk a foot or two high.

Sundews employ a different tactic. As their name suggests, their leaves are covered with gland-tipped hairs that exude a sticky dewlike substance (the genus name, *Drosera*, means "dewy" in Greek). Insects caught by these hairs fight to escape, a strategy that often backfires since adjacent hairs sense movement and respond by helping to hold the struggling animal. The trapped animal is then broken down by digestive enzymes secreted by the glands.

Three species of sundews are found on Long Island: the round-leaved, spatulate- or intermediate-leaved, and the thread-leaved, the rarest of the group. They are easy to tell apart based on the shape of their leaves.

Sundews usually produce a single flowering stalk that emerges from the middle of a rosette of leaves. The stalk produces about six five-petaled flowers that only open in sunshine. In the thread-leaved sundew, the flowers are purple. They are white to pink in the other two species.

Sundews prefer wet, sandy, acid habitats where the water table is close to the surface. Because of these specific habitat requirements, the three sundews have a restricted distribution on Long Island. They are most common along the edges of ponds and in open, sandy bog situations, often growing in association with cranberries, clubmosses and a variety of wildflowers, sedges and rushes.

Bladderworts grow "below" the sundews in standing water along the shallow edges of the pondshore. There are a half dozen or so species native to Long Island, and all but one, which has purple blossoms, have distinctive bright yellow flowers. The flowers of all species have two prominent lips, an upper and a larger lower one which looks like the bottom lip of a pouting child. Bladderworts can be common in the proper habitat, and the blooming of hundreds or thousands of their flowers adds a showy splash of color to the pondshore.

Bladderworts feed upon small animals, primarily tiny aquatic crustaceans. Each plant contains dozens and sometimes hundreds of tiny bladders in the floating, filamentous leaves that hold the plant up. Each bladder has a trap door which opens inward in response to pressure or movement. If the pressure is caused by an animal, it is drawn in and digested. The genus name, *Utricularia*, means small bottle, in reference to the entrapping bladders of this interesting group of plants.

The Venus fly-trap, perhaps the most well-known of the insectivorous plants, captures prey by closing two pads which have interlocking marginal thorns. It is not native to Long Island, however, but is found in suitable wetland environments in southeastern North Carolina and coastal South Carolina.

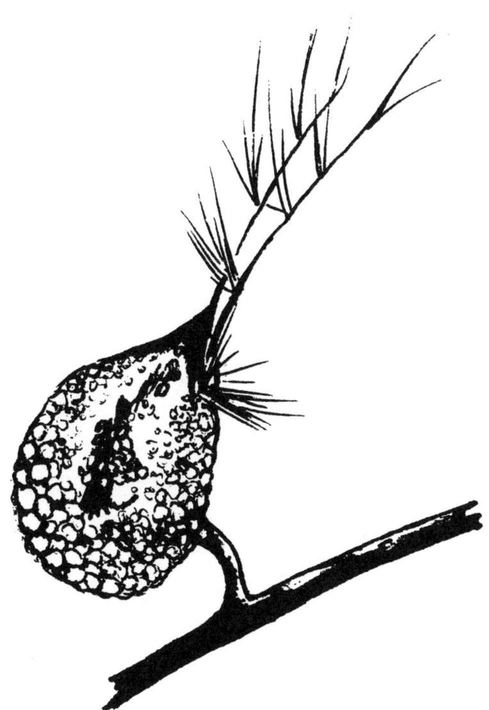

ENTRAPPING BLADDER OF BLADDERWORT, *magnified.* (Susan Spinney)

Coastal Plain Pondshores

The bladderworts and sundews discussed here are part of a natural community which has recently been recognized by ecologists as something special: a coastal plain pondshore.

Many ponds on Long Island are fairly deep, having been formed in glacial basins with typically steep sides. In these ponds a rise or drop in the water table causes little change in the position of the pondshore. Not so with a coastal plain pond which is characteristically shallow; here a foot or two difference in elevation results in a significant change in the shoreline area that is exposed or inundated. As a result, these shorelines have proven to be dynamic places with species composition changing from year to year, depending on water levels.

These pondshores have been identified as one of the most ecologically significant habitats on Long Island and in New York State. For example, more than two dozen rare plants and animals have been found in these pondshore communities. Several are globally rare, such as quill-leaved arrowhead and drowned beak-rush. More common constituents of these communities, in addition to the carnivorous plants previously discussed, include golden hedge-hyssop, comb-leaved mermaid weed, marsh St. Johnswort and rose coreopsis.

The pondshore environment is very fragile and is highly susceptible to trampling by hikers, horses and the scourge and bane of natural areas, the ubiquitous All-Terrain Vehicle. Robert Cushman Murphy County Park in Manorville has the greatest concentration of coastal plain ponds on Long Island.

Where To See Carnivorous Plants

Pitcher plants, sundews and bladderworts are found in a variety of places on Long Island, but given the difference in habitat requirements between pitcher plants and the other two, they rarely grow together or in close proximity. Please note that these plants are protected by law and PICKING IS STRICTLY FORBIDDEN.

For PITCHER PLANTS:

Quogue Wildlife Refuge — some plants grow on the west side of the pond adjacent to the boardwalk that crosses over the pond.

Cranberry Bog County Nature Preserve — pitcher plants grow in several areas in the park, particularly along the edges of the former cranberry bogs.

For **SUNDEWS AND BLADDERWORTS:**

Robert C. Murphy County Park — there are several areas in this park where these two groups of plants grow, either by themselves or together, including:

- Along the eastern edge of the cranberry bogs stretching south of River Road;
- Along the edges of Fox and Sandy Ponds accessed off Line Road or Old River Road. Some of this area is owned by The Nature Conservancy, and you will need to gain permission; call the Long Island Chapter at (516) 367-3225;

- Along the pondshores in the northern reaches of the Park including Sandy (not the same Sandy Pond as the one near Line Road), Peasy's, Woodchopper's, Round and Horn Ponds.

Cranberry Bog County Nature Preserve — both species occur along the edge of Swezey's Pond; sundews are also found in the low-lying woodland adjacent to the pond.

Napeague State Park — sundews grow in the linear cranberry bogs situated in the southern part of the park, north of Montauk Highway.

Key Times

Pitcher plants: the pitcher-shaped leaves can be seen year-round (when not covered by ice or snow); the flowers bloom from late June through early to mid-July

Sundews and **bladderworts:** sundew leaves are visible most of the year. Bladderworts are only recognizable when flowering. Both bloom in early to mid-July.

CHAPTER SEVENTEEN

COMMON DOLPHIN. (Robert T. McGrath)

The Waters Around Us

WHALES AND OTHER MARINE ANIMALS

It had been quiet on the boat since the last whale surfaced several minutes before, bringing with it the usual assortment of "oohs" and "ahs." Abruptly, about fifty feet off the starboard side, a minke whale appeared. It was "spyhopping" — raising its head out of the water to take a look around. People rushed to the corner of the boat to get a better look at the accommodating cetacean, before it slipped back into its watery realm.

Such is the experience of a whale watcher off the Long Island coast. Depending on the time of year, one may see several whale and dolphin species, perhaps a sea turtle or the huge basking shark, and occasionally the ungainly, wonderful looking ocean sunfish, also known as the mola-mola. Pelagic birds provide additional enjoyment, with as many as a dozen species slipping in and out of view as they effortlessly negotiate the peaks and troughs of Atlantic Ocean waves.

But whales are the main attraction. The most common is the fin or **finback whale** which is named for its large dorsal fin. This large whale can reach up to eighty feet in length and weigh close to fifty tons (although most are somewhat smaller). The species is identified by the distinctive chevron mark behind the blowhole, and individuals are recognizable by differences in the shape and outline of their chevron. Interestingly, finbacks are asymmetrically colored, with the jaw being white on the right side of the animal's head and black on the left. Scientists are still not sure why the whale is so uniquely patterned.

A resident population of several hundred finback whales is strongly suspected of breeding in New York waters. Researchers are growing increasingly convinced of this breeding phenomenon off the east end of Long Island for several reasons. The siting of newborn calves in the area is the most conclusive, given that whale calves are unable to swim long distances after birth and therefore unlikely emigrants from other places.

The **minke whale** (pronounced *mink-ee*) is a smaller cousin of the finback. In fact, it looks a bit like a baby finback, reaching a maximum length of thirty-five feet and weight of eleven tons. It is among the smallest of the baleen whales, animals that feed by straining small marine organisms through a sievelike material known as baleen. Some minkes carry the chevron pattern typical of finbacks.

Humpback whales are occasionally seen off Long Island's coast. Humpbacks are well-known for their beautiful songs which carry for great distances, and for their huge pectoral fins, or flippers, that can be as long as sixteen feet.

They are most well-known, however, for their habit of tail and flipper slapping and breaching, whereby the whale hurls itself virtually out of the water, returning with a resounding splash. Scientists are not sure why they do this; perhaps it is an effort to dislodge parasites, or a form of communication or, the most probable, because it's just plain fun. Seeing a humpback breach is a sight not soon forgotten.

Other baleen whale species that are only seldom seen include the blue whale, the largest whale in the world, and the right whale, one of the most endangered. The sperm whale of Moby Dick fame, a toothed whale, is also rarely present.

Several species of **dolphins** and porpoises play in the waters off Long Island. These include the beautifully patterned common, bottle-nosed, spotted, white-sided and striped dolphins and the harbor porpoises.

In addition to marine mammals, a number of sea turtle species can be seen, including the largest and most ocean-going of all turtle species: the **leatherback.** Looking like a large piece of black, rubbery armor, this species may reach lengths of nine feet and weigh up to three-quarters of a ton. As its name suggests, the leatherback lacks a hard, bony top shell. Rather, it is covered by thick leathery skin with seven long ridges which give the animal a beautifully streamlined appearance. Many large white to pink-colored spots cover the shell and prominent front flippers. The turtle feeds exclusively on jellyfish, and several die each year after mistaking plastic bags or balloons for their dinner (one reason why many marine biologists would like to see lighter-than-air balloon launches halted).

Underscoring its oceangoing nature, the leatherback has evolved without the ability to turn while in water. In its natural open ocean habitat it has no reason to. Captive individuals, however, have been known to die from infected abrasions caused by rubbing against a tank wall in a futile effort to move forward.

As one sets out on the first leg of a whale watching trip, when the boat is but a few miles off the coast, typical water birds such as gulls and terns are still common. As the boat moves further out into the Atlantic Ocean though, these species drop away and you begin to see birds unknown to the landlubber.

The **Wilson's storm-petrel,** a swallow-sized bird, is the first to pass near the boat. With its white rump patch appearing in marked contrast to the generally sooty-colored body, and its diagnostic flight behavior of dipping and puttering over the water, there is no mistaking its identification.

Out beyond the storm-petrel your eye may focus on two larger birds: the **greater** and **Cory's shearwaters.** Gull-size birds with narrow wings, the shearwaters skirt over the wave tops in a stiff-winged flight, looking as if they might shear the water at any moment. The Cory's is rather nondescript (which ironically assists in its identification), while the greater has an attractive black cap and tail with a distinctive white tail band.

Shearwaters and storm petrels often congregate near feeding finbacks, drawn to their prey which often includes small fish such as sand launce (also known as sand eels).

Other birds to be seen include the northern gannet, northern fulmar, phalaropes, skua, several species of jaegers and other species of storm-petrels and shearwaters.

Where to See Marine Animals

You may see some of the above-mentioned species on any oceangoing fishing boat. However, to increase your chances you are strongly urged to go out on one of the scheduled daily whale watching trips sponsored by the Okeanos Ocean Research Foundation (516-728-4522) that leave from Montauk Harbor. These trips run from late May through September.

Autumn

NORTHERN HARRIER. (Maria T. Weisenberg)

LESSER YELLOW LEGS. (Marc Oliveri)

CHAPTER EIGHTEEN
Southbound Shorebirds

Shorebirds fly vast distances on strong, efficient wings to reach breeding and wintering grounds separated by thousands of miles. Their various whistles and calls have been described as plaintive, evocative and haunting. They feed in areas which are exposed and uncompromising, battered by rain and buffeted by wind: mudflats, salt pans, marsh, bay edges and tidal pools.

To watch a flock of sandpipers or a small group of yellowlegs drop from the autumn sky with bodies and wings twisting in response to millisecond changes in aerodynamic conditions; to listen to their lonely, compelling calls is to experience utter wildness. The birds carry with them the desolation of tundra.

Beginning as early as mid- to late July and running through late October and beyond, a number of shorebird species appear on Long Island's coast, fresh from their northern nesting grounds. Their numbers usually peak in early to mid-September. They feed incessantly to gain the fuel necessary to carry them on to their final wintering destinations in the southeastern United States, the Caribbean and various regions of South America (a few species reach Tierra del Fuego at the continent's southern tip). The adults arrive several weeks before the more brightly colored, fresh-plumaged, "hatchyear" juveniles.

The "peep" sandpipers are especially common. Hard to identify due to their similarity, the **least** and **semipalmated** (so named because its feet are slightly webbed) **sandpipers** are small and brownish in color with prominent, chisel-shaped bills. In good light conditions these two species can be differentiated: the least has yellow legs while those of the semipalmated are dark colored, as are those of other peep sandpipers. Birders use a popular mnemonic device to tell the least apart from the other peeps: "The least has light legs." Less commonly seen peep sandpipers include the white-rumped (the white crescent is quite visible in flight), the Baird's and the western with its characteristic, slightly drooping bill.

Not to be confused with the semipalmated sandpiper is the rather common **semipalmated plover** (also with slightly webbed feet). A handsome brown bird with a short orange bill, a single black neck band and golden yellow legs and feet, the semipalmated is closely related to the piping plover which nests on Long Island's beaches (see Chapter 3). The **killdeer,** with its call that sounds like *"kill-deer,"* is also brown, but has a bright orange tail and two dark breast bands. Killdeer nest in short grass areas such as soccer fields throughout Long Island.

Another plover, the **black-bellied plover,** appears in large numbers during fall migration. Early in the season individuals in breeding plumage are common: checkered black-and-white back, white neck and shoulder stripe, and solid black belly, cheek and throat. Their haunting, slurred-whistle call sounds like *"where? where? where?"*

The **sanderling,** a peeplike shorebird, can be distinguished from the true peeps by its chunkier appearance and (in the fall) lighter, uniform plumage. Also, they are most often seen feeding along the outer beach and less often in other habitats. As the froth of a wave moves up the beach, the birds retreat before it, then advance to look for food particles as the wave slides back down.

Ruddy turnstones, some of which are still in their distinctive harlequin breeding plumage when they arrive on Long Island, received their names from their habit of turning over stones, driftwood and other debris in search of food. They are among the most colorful of shorebirds.

Two species of yellowlegs move through Long Island on fall migration. The **lesser yellowlegs** is about ten inches long and has a thin, straight bill. Its cousin, the **greater yellowlegs,** is a few inches larger and has a proportionately longer bill that is slightly upturned. They are most easily told apart by their call: the lesser emits a two syllable *"tew-tew"* call, while the greater issues a more piercing, triple syllable *"tew-tew-tew."*

The two species of dowitchers are also difficult to tell apart. However, since **short-billed dowitchers** arrive from the north before the **long-billed,** any dowitchers seen early in the fall season are of the former species. Dowitchers can be distinguished from other shorebirds by their unique feeding behavior. They rapidly move their long, straight bills up and down in a sewing machine motion, as they probe vertically in the mud of the marshes and flats they inhabit.

Each year brings reports of several of the **larger shorebird species** such as Hudsonian godwits, whimbrels, and larger still, marbled godwits and avocets. Mingling on a mudflat, these birds dwarf their smaller shorebird cousins. The whimbrel has a distinctive sickle-shaped bill that is downcurved, while the other three have straight or upturned (recurved) bills.

Most of these shorebirds breed much further north than Long Island, many in the Arctic tundra, but two shorebirds in addition to the piping plover breed here: the **oystercatcher** and the **willet.** Given its large size, black-and-white pattern, yellow eye, and large, chisel-shaped, bright red bill (it uses its bill to break open oysters, mussels and other shellfish that are its primary food), the oystercatcher is not likely to be confused with any other bird. It nests on several islands in the south shore bays and along undisturbed stretches of the barrier beach, occasionally in association with tern and piping plover colonies.

Standing in a salt marsh, the nondescript willet is easy to overlook. But let it take flight, and it is unmistakable. Its bold black-and-white wings, heretofore tucked out of sight, flash conspicuously, and it often calls out its plaintive, namesake call, "*will, will, willet? will, will, willet?*" (In my case, the call of the willet invariably triggers pleasant memories of summer days spent at Long Island's seashores.)

THE "GRASSPIPERS"

The majority of shorebirds frequent mudflats, shallow pools, tidal wetlands and sandy beaches to feed — hence the common name, sandpiper. The **upland** and **buff-breasted sandpipers,** however, are more at home walking through a sod farm than a mudflat. Because of their preference for grassy areas, birders often refer to them as the "grasspipers."

The upland sandpiper was once a common breeding bird on the Hempstead Plains (see Chapter 10) and still breeds in a few locations on Long Island where suitable grassland habitat remains. Also, breeding populations from the northern United States and southern Canada pass through on their southbound migration. In contrast, the buff-breasted sandpiper breeds in the high arctic of northwestern Canada, and the only time of year it is reliably seen on Long Island is during autumn migration.

The birds are similar in appearance. Both have a "small-headed" look, dark eyes and scaly backs. The upland sandpiper is larger and darkly colored. The underside of the buff-breasted is, as its name suggests, a rich buffy color, somewhat the color of a robin's breast that has gone through too many cycles in the washing machine. Both walk with a distinctive upright posture.

Besides being similar in appearance and in their choice of foraging habitat used during fall migration, the birds also choose similar wintering habitat. They overwinter together in the grasslands of Uruguay and Argentina. Their annual round-trip migration from breeding grounds to wintering grounds is among the longest of any bird. Unfortunately, these southern grasslands are following the example set by our own: they are being converted into fields of wheat, corn and other crops. Not surprisingly, these two wonderful birds, which epitomize open, windswept landscapes, are declining rapidly. Some scientists fear they may become extinct in our lifetime.

Where to See Shorebirds

Shorebirds can be seen in suitable habitat along most of Long Island's interdigitated coastline. There are several places, however, where you are virtually guaranteed to see the shorebird species discussed above.

Jamaica Bay Wildlife Refuge — off Cross Bay Boulevard in southern Brooklyn is one of the premier sites for viewing shorebirds. The east pond is particularly worthwhile, where refuge officials manage water levels to expose an ample amount of pond margin for the birds to use. Many rare species such as the ruff and the curlew sandpiper (European shorebirds) turn up regularly each fall.

Cow Meadow Park — Freeport, southern Nassau County, is another site to see shorebirds. The birds use pools that can be viewed from a nearby nature trail or viewing tower, both of which are situated south of the parking lot.

Overlook Beach — along the Ocean Parkway in Babylon is an outstanding site to view plovers and sandpipers. While you are supposed to be a town resident to gain access to the park, the town graciously allows birders from throughout Long Island to visit the park in the fall. The best location for viewing shorebirds is a pool that is a ten-minute walk east of the pavilion.

Many sections of ocean beach such as **Jones Beach** and **Fire Island State Parks, Fire Island National Seashore,** and **Smith Point County Park** provide opportunities to see flocks of sanderlings.

The section of Shinnecock Bay shoreline on the north side of the barrier beach and on each side of the **Ponquogue Bridge** in Hampton Bays can be rewarding for shorebirds. A large mussel bed immediately to the west of the bridge, easily viewed during low tide from **Dune Road,** is a reliable location for oystercatchers. This area is also worthwhile for some of the other shorebird species mentioned. A ride west along Dune Road takes you past stretches of tidal marsh that fringe Shinnecock Bay. Here willets are a "shore" bet.

For **"GRASSPIPERS":**

During the breeding season upland sandpipers can be found on Long Island in areas with extensive grasslands. **Floyd Bennett Field,** part of the **Gateway National Recreation Area** in southern Brooklyn, on the east side of Flatbush Avenue south of the Belt Parkway, and the **Suffolk County Airport** in Westhampton are among the places where upland sandpipers can be reliably seen. You might still be lucky enough to see a bird or two at the **Hempstead Plains Preserve** in Uniondale.

Migrating upland and buff-breasted sandpipers are reliably seen in three areas on eastern Long Island: in the open fields both north and south of the intersection of Sunrise Highway and County Route 51 in the south Manorville/ Eastport area; the sod farms situated north of the hamlet of Riverhead in the vicinity of Doctor's Path and County Route 105; and in Cutchogue, on the North Fork, near Alvah's Lane and Oregon Road.

Key times

Southbound shorebird migration can start as early as late July, but numbers do not pick up usually until early to mid-August. The abundance and diversity of shorebirds peaks in the month from late August through the last week in September. Good numbers of late arriving groups sometimes persist into late October and early November.

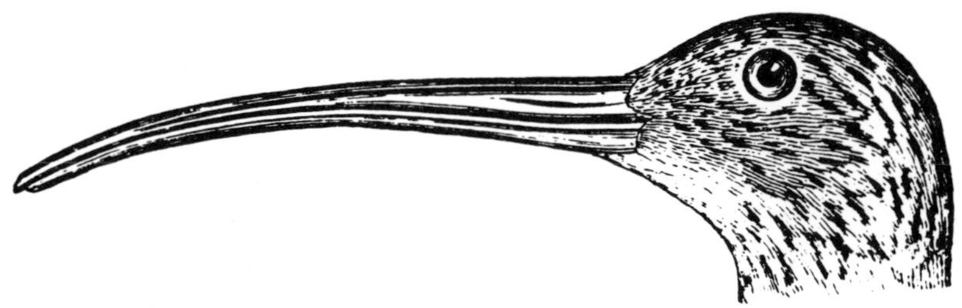

WHIMBREL. (From *The Water Birds of North America,* by Baird, Brewer, Ridgway)

MERLIN. (Marc Oliveri)

CHAPTER NINETEEN

Hawks Above the Dunes

The sharp-shinned hawk first appeared as a speck on the horizon, but with a twenty-mile-per-hour westerly tailwind it came on fast. The bird cut in front of the Fire Island Lighthouse and headed toward the bay until, turning abruptly by throwing its flight and tail feathers forward in a breaking action, it darted south into a stand of black pine. It left the viewers at the Fire Island hawk watch amazed at its aerial ability.

A few minutes later another bird, also but a speck on the horizon, flew with strong deliberate wing beats, making up ground even faster than did the sharp-shinned hawk. It did not waver as it approached the observers, who realized they were watching a merlin, a medium-sized falcon and one of the fastest flyers in the bird world. But to their surprise the merlin did not continue its arrow-straight flight along the dunes. As it came even with the watchers, it broke back into the wind and dove upon an unsuspecting crow, turning away inches from the surprised bird. Again, the watchers expressed their awe at this bird's command of the air.

These birds of prey, or raptors, were but two of several thousand birds that move along Long Island's south shore barrier beaches each autumn during migration. (From 1987 to 1992 an annual average of 4,930 hawks passed by the hawk watch.) Their southbound, migratory journeys are timed to match the migration of their prey, the passerines, or songbirds, such as warblers, vireos, flycatchers and sparrows.

The migration of raptors is particularly heavy along the south shore of Long Island, due to the hawks' taste for open expanses and ample food supplies. It probably is also in response to the barrier the Atlantic Ocean poses to a southbound bird. Many birds, raptors included, will shun large bodies of water and instead of flying across them, although it may be the shorter route, will follow the coast. Raptors, traversing the Island on their way south, meet the Atlantic and turn west, opting to follow the coastline. This is not always true, however, since hawk watchers have often seen merlins and peregrine falcons reach Democrat Point, the westernmost tip of Fire Island, and turn out to sea at a forty-five degree angle. These birds presumably are taking a shortcut across the New York Bight, heading for the New Jersey coastline.

More than half a dozen species of raptors can be seen with regularity during fall migration along the Island's south shore: accipiters, including sharp-shinned and Cooper's hawks; falcons, including the kestrel (formerly known as the sparrow hawk), merlin (formerly known as the pigeon hawk), and the reigning king of the bird's of prey, the peregrine falcon; the osprey; and the northern harrier or marsh hawk.

The birds begin to move through in early September and continue through late October, though peak time is from mid-September to mid-October. During this time the Fire Island hawk watch is staffed by a cadre of friendly, trained and dedicated observers with the skill to identify the various species.

Weather plays a key role in influencing raptor flight, with the exception of merlins and peregrine falcons which are such strong flyers that light rain and wind are largely irrelevant. The best or heaviest flight days occur when a ten- to fifteen-mile-per-hour wind blows from the north or northwest (often associated with a passing cold front). Generally the earlier in the morning the wind begins, the better the flight. Flights are also heavy following several days of inclement weather, when large numbers of "pent-up" hawks move through.

The **American Kestrel,** or "AK" as it is referred to by the hawk watchers, has been the most common raptor every year since the hawk watch began in 1982. In a single day (October 1, 1987, to be precise) two observers counted 1,386 kestrels.

Since kestrels nest on Long Island, they can be seen in other seasons as well. The autumn birds are not part of Long Island's breeding population, but are individuals from more northerly regions. The observant driver can occasionally see kestrels hunting (characteristically hovering in place with rapid wing beats as they search the ground below them for prey) along the shoulders and medians of Long Island's major roadways, including the Long Island Expressway and Sunrise Highway. Kestrels nest in tree cavities and will use nesting boxes.

Migrating **merlins** and **peregrine falcons** are birds from more northerly areas; in the case of peregrines from as far away as Greenland.

Although the merlin is generally the second most abundant bird along the south shore, with slightly more than 1,000 birds seen each fall, it is the "bread and butter" bird of the hawk watch. During the fifty-nine day field season in 1991, for example, only five days went by without any merlins rocketing past the watch. In contrast, the kestrel, the most common but only second most predictable raptor, skunked the watchers eleven times.

The peregrine falcon can be as predictable as the other two falcons if you visit the hawk watch during the first two weeks of October. Of the 168 peregrines counted in 1991, 112, or sixty-six percent, passed through in a twelve-day period from October 1-12. The one-day record for peregrines stands at forty-nine birds and was recorded on October 2, 1989.

The **sharp-shinned hawk** belongs to the group of hawks known as accipiters (sometimes called the bird or forest hawks). Their short, broad wings and long tails enable them to fly through the forest in pursuit of avian prey. An average of about 800 sharp-shinned hawks pass through the hawk watch each fall. The sharp-shinned is an uncommon breeding bird on Long Island.

The **northern harrier** (or marsh hawk as it is commonly called) is another raptor which passes through the hawk watch, though in fewer numbers than the previously mentioned species. In 1991, 131 birds flew by. It is also an uncommon breeding bird on Long Island, but due to size, distinctive flight behavior, and the open country it inhabits, the harrier can be seen from spring through fall on most car trips along the Ocean Parkway.

The **buteos** or soaring hawks, such as the red-tailed or broad-winged hawk, do not migrate along the coast, preferring instead to use updrafts and thermals created along mountain ridges to aid their migration south. Both species breed on Long Island, however, and may be seen during the warmer months in appropriate habitat.

Other Hawk Watching Sites

For the adventurous, there are several other places to watch hawks. Cape May, a three-and-a-half-hour ride away, at the southern tip of New Jersey, is internationally renowned for its autumnal flights of falcons, accipiters and other raptors. Live raptor demonstrations sponsored by the Cape May Bird Observatory take place on weekends in the fall. There are many fine restaurants, bed & breakfast establishments, and Victorian homes in Cape May to be enjoyed.

Hawk Mountain in eastern central Pennsylvania, about four hours away, has an entirely different flavor than Cape May, and a different group of hawks as well. Here, on suitable days, you can see "kettles" of hawks, involving hundreds of birds, as they circle on warm, uprising thermal currents. Bald eagles pass by with regularity. From the mountain top lookout, about a three-quarter mile walk from the parking lot, you have a commanding view of the adjacent valleys and a great place to enjoy the changing fall colors. Staff naturalists in the visitor's center and at the lookouts are on hand to answer questions.

Closer to home, about two hours away, are the hawk watches at the Butler Sanctuary on Chestnut Ridge Road (which is off Route 172, which in turn is Exit 4 off Route 684) in Westchester County, and at Hook Mountain on the west side of the Hudson River, several miles north of the Tappan Zee Bridge.

Where to See Hawks

As you have obviously concluded, the Fire Island hawk watch is an ideal place to watch migrating birds of prey. The hawk watch is situated at the eastern end of **Robert Moses State Park,** west of the Fire Island Lighthouse. To get to the hawk watch take the causeway bridge to the state park, make a three-quarter circle around the tower, and head east on the parkway. Take the road to parking field #5, and park in the eastern section of the lot (there is a parking fee). Walk east along the grassy shoulder of the road to where the road loops back west. At this point you will see two large red-and-white traffic barriers and people with binoculars, all suffering from "hawk fever," a wonderful affliction for which there is no cure, except a regular dose of hawks whizzing by the dunes.

While the hawk watch is ideal since it is staffed with knowledgeable birders, there are other places to see hawks. Other sections of **Robert Moses State Park** west to Democrat Point can be productive, as can all of **Jones Beach State Park.**

As described above, harriers can be regularly seen, rocking back and forth in their unique hunting flight, over the **Ocean Parkway** which bisects Jones Beach. Kestrels can often be seen hunting along major Long Island highways, and it is not unusual to see red-tailed hawks sitting on top of the light poles of the **Northern** and **Southern State Parkways.**

BUCKEYE AND MONARCH BUTTERFLIES ON SEASIDE GOLDENROD. (Marc Oliveri)

CHAPTER TWENTY
Other Animals Migratory

Birds of prey may be the best-known fall-migrants along the Island's south shore barrier beach, but by no means are they the only animals to be seen on an autumn visit there. Often migration along the beach seems like a parade of migratory animal species. Birds such as flickers, kinglets and tree swallows move through; a variety of insects including monarch, buckeye and red admiral butterflies pass by with fluttered determination; assorted dragonfly species zoom back and forth as they wind westward along the beach. They all are moved by the same impulse to head south with the approach of winter cold.

On some fall mornings a trip to the barrier beach borders on the magical. A visit the day before had been quiet, but today, seemingly out of nowhere, there are thousands of **northern flickers** (a ground-loving woodpecker) feeding along the grassy shoulders of Ocean Parkway and adjacent roads. The flicker is distinguished by the brown-and-black barring on the back, black spotting on the breast, stomach and sides, prominent black chest collar and red mark on the back of the head. Males have an additional black mustache mark.

Like most woodpeckers, flickers fly in an easily recognized, undulating pattern. They take a few flaps and then pull in their wings, causing them to drop; they flap again to gain elevation, and repeat the cycle. This flight behavior, illustrated in other birds such as the goldfinches, is thought to save energy, which is not a bad strategy, particularly during migration.

The northern flicker is a common breeding bird on Long Island, so an observer need not wait until autumn to see one. Actually, flickers are more often heard than seen. Their disconcerting call has been likened to the cry of a madman loose in the woods. Listen for it in a forest near you!

Golden-crowned kinglets also seem to appear overnight. Where the day before there were no kinglets, today there are thousands of the little mites covering the grassy shoulders of Ocean Parkway. Sometimes you can approach to within a few feet of them, and occasionally they may be picked up, due to exhaustion caused by the rigors of migration (although out of concern for the bird you are advised not to do so).

Due to flocking behavior, it is easy to tell when **tree swallows** have begun their migration. The bird changes from a solitary nester to a gregarious peregrinator. They can be seen by the hundreds perching along power lines. Flocks occasionally number in the thousands, thereby making the tree swallow one of the most abundant autumn migrants along the Island's south shore. The iridescence of their blue-green feathers gives the birds a metallic look as they sweep back and forth searching for insect food.

A number of other bird species, in lesser abundance, can be found by searching the hedgerows and pine thickets along the barrier beach. These include a variety of warblers, vireos, sparrows, thrushes, cuckoos and flycatchers. Every year an exotic species or two from such faraway places as northern Europe or western Asia turns up here to bring additional excitement to the life of the bird watcher.

Fall migration generally brings to mind the strong, purposeful flight of southbound birds, but one common migrant along the beach is more of a flutterer than a flyer. It is the **monarch butterfly.** From mid-September through early November (in warm years), these beautiful orange-and-black butterflies float along the barrier beach in steady numbers. There is something about their fragile appearance that brings to mind a rickety old jalopy, limping along the Long Island Expressway with a brazen boast taped to its rear, "Mexico or Bust!" From all appearances, one doubts that the next exit is achievable, let alone a multi-thousand-mile journey. But the wintering roost of the monarch butterfly, now made famous by pictures showing hundreds of thousands of butterflies draping individual trees, consists of a relatively small area of montane forest in the Sierra Madre Mountains of central Mexico.

Along the way the insects stop to rest and feed upon the nectar produced by seaside goldenrod that blooms during the fall. In normal years, upwards of a half-dozen individuals can be seen feeding on a single plant.

As with migrating birds, Long Island seems to be a funnel for migrating monarch butterflies emanating from New England and maritime Canada. Flying south, they reach Long Island only to be deterred by the open ocean. They therefore follow the land, moving west along the south shore.

Unfortunately, this most famous of all butterflies seems to be in trouble. Many Long Island naturalists noticed that the 1992 fall flight was the lightest in years. Only six or seven individuals were seen some days, in marked contrast to the usual tally in the hundreds. The causes offered to explain this significant drop in numbers range from continued destruction of habitat within its breeding range (throughout eastern North America), continued use of pesticides, and perhaps most importantly, the destruction of the woodlands that are home to its wintering colonies.

The wintering grounds in the Sierra Madre are protected by the Mexican government, but because of the local people's need for fuel, the groves are still cut. Entomologists fear that even if the specific trees the butterflies use for roosting are left intact, the cutting of adjacent forests may change the microclimate of the area to a degree that it can no longer support the overwintering butterflies.

Monarchs are not the only invertebrates that can be seen migrating along the barrier beach. Other butterflies to look out for are the buckeye, the painted lady, its cousin, the red admiral, and the variegated fritillary. Also present, occasionally in large numbers, is the green darner dragonfly.

THE COMMON NIGHTHAWK: DANCERS IN THE SKY

A sure sign that summer is growing long in the tooth is the southward passage of the common nighthawk. Although the nighthawk breeds on Long Island, the birds seen darting and dancing in the sky from late August through mid-September are migratory birds that have nested in more northerly locations.

Their flight behavior is quite distinctive. Strong fliers, nighthawks easily cut the air on falcon-shaped wings, but the erratic ballet they perform makes one think they can never quite make up their mind which way to go. In reality, the birds know exactly where they are going — they are heading to their South American wintering grounds. Along the way they feed on a variety of aerial insects. This habit of feeding in flight gives credence to one of the nighthawk's other names: the flying mouth.

Field marks, in addition to the bird's distinctive flight pattern, are the prominent: white stripes that cross the underside of the wing, and which visibly flash as the nighthawk pirouettes overhead. The combination of flight behavior and tell-tale underwing striping is foolproof evidence that you are watching a common nighthawk.

The nighthawk is crepuscular, meaning that it is most active toward dawn and dusk. Those migrating over Long Island are most often seen at these times. They can also be seen after dark, flitting around the light stanchions illuminating late-summer softball games. It is not so much their love of softball that brings them, but the large numbers of insects that are attracted to the bright lights. They come, to paraphrase the famous bank robber, Willy Sutton, because that is where the bugs are.

While single birds often pass through, groups of three or four are most common. On one occasion I saw eight birds dancing together over the Sunrise Highway in Oakdale. I immediately pulled over to enjoy the display of their intertwining flight lines. These numbers pale beside the migratory flocks of yesteryear, which often involved more than one hundred birds. One flock was estimated to contain nearly 1,000 birds.

The nighthawk is closely related to the whip-poor-will and the chuck-will's-widow, all being members of the goatsucker family. (The latter two species breed on Long Island.) This strange family name evolves from the false, but once common, belief that these big-mouthed birds would attach to the teats of livestock to feed.

Where To See Other Migratory Animals

The species described above can be seen at the same parks mentioned in the chapter on migrating hawks. These include the **Jamaica Bay Wildlife Refuge,** the various units of the **Gateway National Recreational Area** such as **Floyd Bennett Field, Breezy Point** and **Jacob Riis Park; Jones Beach** and **Robert Moses State Parks;** and **Fire Island National Seashore** (particularly the more accessible western half); and **Smith Point County Park.**

Key Times

On pleasant days from the middle of September through early November the migratory species mentioned above should be present.

BUCK MOTH, FEMALE. (John F. Cryan)

CHAPTER TWENTY-ONE

Flight of the Buck Moth

As the monarch butterfly has come to symbolize the arrival of autumn along our barrier beach, the buck moth heralds the season in the Pine Barrens. For when the black huckleberry that carpets the open heaths of the Pine Barrens turns scarlet, the buck moth emerges on the scene.

A beautifully patterned, white, black and orange insect with a wingspan of one and a half inches, the adult buck moth emerges for a two-week period in mid-October, the time of year when white-tailed deer bucks were hunted, and hence the name. It is most active during late morning through mid-afternoon. During this time male moths can be seen zipping between pitch pines, searching for the scent trail of a female. Meanwhile, she will be hanging from a scrub oak twig, emitting a sex attractant known as a pheromone.

Male moths, differentiated from females by their bright orange abdomen tufts and feathery antennae (compared with the female's dull-colored abdomen and wiry antennae), are quite adept at picking up the scent. Moreover, they can sense slight changes in the concentration of the windborne chemical, thereby learning in which direction to fly to find the emitting female.

After mating, the female lays up to 200 eggs in a tight cluster on a scrub oak branch (the cluster resembles the tiny corn-on-the-cob found in Chinese vegetables). She will then die, as will the male. Having no mouth parts enabling them to feed, the adults die when their food supply (stored energy in the form of body fat that was carried over from the caterpillar stage) gives out.

The insect overwinters in the egg stage. The eggs hatch in early May. Feeding on the emerging scrub oak leaves (its primary host plant), the quarter-inch-long caterpillars grow quickly. Initially, they band together to gain protection in numbers from predators such as birds. Small masses feed together on the same leaves. But as they grow and develop spines formidable enough to deter birds, they split into smaller groups. This strategy prevents the larger group from succumbing to a parasite or pathogen. Finally, after six growth stages called instars, the caterpillar's growth is complete. It has reached two inches long, is a pretty mustard-and-black color, and is armed with rows of urticating (stinging) spines.

Instinct, or some genetically coded caterpillar thought, then guides the caterpillar downward from the scrub oak into the sandy ground. Here, in late July, several inches below the pine-littered surface, the caterpillar undergoes the magical transformation from caterpillar to adult moth.

Why does the buck moth have the strange habit of pupating underground, especially when its closely related silk moth cousins, such as the polyphemus, cecropia and luna moths, pupate in a cocoon suspended from a branch? It has to do with wildfire.

The buck moth has evolved to survive in dry, sandy habitats like the Pine Barrens which owe their existence to regular and sometimes intense wildfire. If the moth developed a pupa which hung from a branch, it would likely be destroyed by fire, and the species would not survive. So, in the fullness of time, the buck moth evolved a strategy that worked: insulated by inches of soil, the pupa is out of harm's way during the period when it is most vulnerable, and the outbreak of wildfire is most likely.

Through the summer the pupa remains beneath the surface, awaiting the cooler rains of fall. If they occur on schedule, metamorphosis is initiated, and the adult moths break out in mid-October. A dry spell in late summer probably means the pupa will wait out a year until rains occur the following fall. Buck moth pupa have been known to live for several years underground if conditions do not trigger metamorphosis.

Emergence takes several hours to complete. Pumping straw-colored blood through its body, the moth slowly unfurls its wings. The cycle closes when the males fly off in search of a female, and she climbs a twig in search of a male.

THE LONG ISLAND DWARF PINE PLAINS

The Long Island Pine Barrens is a mosaic of many different types of forests. Perhaps the rarest is the globally rare Dwarf Pine Plains, situated in Westhampton. Encompassing about 2,500 acres, it is bisected by Sunrise Highway and County Route 31, thereby forming four quadrants. The Suffolk County Airport takes up much of the southeast quadrant.

The Dwarf Pine Plains is named after a dwarf form of pitch pine which rarely grows taller than shoulder height. In some areas the pines often do not reach above the waist. Some naturalists have likened the area to an oriental bonsai garden; in this case a garden about four square miles in size. The main trunk and limbs of the dwarf pines are often twisted and contorted, adding to the oriental flair. A clear understanding of the factors that led to the establishment and perpetuation of this unique forest type does not yet exist.

Timothy Dwight, a theologian and past president of Yale University, writing in his 1822 *Travels in New England and New York*, had this to say about the Dwarf Pine Plains: "Not far from this hamlet is a spot of ground about three miles in diameter, which, as I was informed by good authority, is covered with shrub oaks and pines, not more than five or six feet in height. In the whole tract there is not a single tree of the usual size, although it is surrounded by a forest of such trees. The cause of this phenomenon in a place where the soil is substantially the same with that of the neighboring country, it is not easy to assign."

The Pine Plains in Westhampton are one of only three such communities known in the world. The others are located in the New Jersey Pine Barrens (actually the New Jersey Dwarf Pine Plains consist of five different areas that are in close proximity) and along the Shawangunk ridge south of the Catskills. Due to their scarcity, the Dwarf Pine Plains are of global significance.

A distinctive feature of these pygmy pines is the high frequency of serotinous, or "closed," pine cones. While pine cones from tree-sized pines open and shed their seeds each year, the cones on the dwarf pines remain closed and will not open to release their seeds unless they are burned. Burning melts the resin which holds the scales closed, allowing the seeds to fall free. (See Chapter 9 for other fire-adapted traits of pitch pines.)

This closed cone feature is thought to be an adaptation that evolved to take advantage of the periodic fires that have strongly affected the pine plains. Due to the low stature of the forest, a fire sweeping through the Dwarf Pine Plains is likely to burn everything above the ground. If the dwarf pines had "normal" open cones, the seeds would probably perish. But by adopting the trait of "closed coneness," the seeds not only survive wildfire, they fall onto a rich,. ashy ground layer, generously bathed in sunlight. These are excellent growing conditions for the pine seedlings.

Birds found in the pine plains include prairie warbler, rufous-sided towhee, brown thrasher, field sparrow, whip-poor-will and, surprisingly, a breeding population of northern harriers, a bird more associated with coastal marshes than with pine barrens. Bearberry, a member of the blueberry family, carpets the floor and blooms in late April. Scrub oak, the host plant of the buck moth, black huckleberry and several blueberries bloom a few weeks later. Many species of lichens grow here as well.

Where To See The Buck Moth

At the right time of year, buck moths can be seen anywhere in the Long Island Pine Barrens. Since it is limited to feeding on scrub oak as a caterpillar, it is more likely to be seen in areas of the Pine Barrens that have an abundance of this oak.

Particularly good areas to find caterpillars or to watch the mating flight include:

The Oak Brush Plains State Preserve — in Brentwood, administered by the New York State Department of Environmental Conservation. The main entrance is situated on the east side of Commack Road about one mile south of the Long Island Expressway.

The South Setauket Pine Barrens — east of Nicoll's Road, including the County's Setauket Conservation Area and the parcels bisected by Terminal Road.

The Dwarf Pine Plains — in Westhampton, intersected by Sunrise Highway and County Route 31. Several trails leading west from Route 31 provide access to the area. According to some authorities, THIS AREA HAS THE GREATEST CONCENTRATION OF BUCK MOTHS IN THE WORLD.

Key Times

For caterpillars, the month of June.

For the moth mating flight, from October 6–20, between 10:00 A.M. and 2:00 P.M.

WITCH HAZEL BUDS AND LEAVES. (National Agricultural Library, Forest Service Photographic Collection)

CHAPTER TWENTY-TWO

Witch Hazel

FLOWERS AT THANKSGIVING

The last goldenrods have died and the few remaining asters have faded and will soon die too. It is a fortnight before Thanksgiving and frost has become a nightly event. However, the blooming season is not yet complete; remarkably, it is just beginning for one plant: witch hazel, or winter-bloom.

Why witch hazel blooms so late in the fall is unclear. It may follow the strategy used by skunk cabbage in the spring, that is, bloom at a time when competition for insect pollinators is significantly reduced, thereby enhancing the likelihood of successful reproduction. The flowers are pollinated by wasps, gnats and several types of flies, all of which may be made scarce by cold weather. To insure against this potential dearth of pollinators, witch hazel flowers can also pollinate themselves. Also, there is some evidence that fertilization of the pollinated flower is delayed until spring (a strategy similar to the delayed implantation seen in a number of mammal species).

Witch hazel flowers are not easily confused with any other shrub. Growing in small clusters at the base of the leaves, the straw-yellow flowers have four, narrow, ribbonlike petals that give the flower cluster the appearance of windblown confetti.

Witch hazel leaves are distinctive as well. The medium-sized leaves have scalloped, roundly toothed edges and prominent parallel veins that extend to the edge. Most interestingly, and for an unknown reason, the leaves are asymmetrical in that the base of the leaf is uneven. As described in Britton and Brown's *Illustrated Flora of the Northeastern United States and Canada*, the leaves are "inequilateral at the broadly rounded or subordinate base." In other words, the bottom of the leafy blades attach at slightly different points along the main stem.

The fruits are woody capsules which release last year's seeds at the same time this year's flowers are in bloom. This unusual arrangement of having flowers and seeds on the plant at the same time lies behind the plant's generic name, *Hamamelis*, meaning "fruit at the same time" in Greek. The seeds are sometimes projected as much as twenty-five feet, giving rise to another colloquial name: snapping alder.

A shrub that sometimes reaches the stature of a small tree, witch hazel generally occurs as an understory tree in moist soil woodlands. On Long Island such woodlands are dominated by black birch, flowering dogwood and various hickory species. It is scattered throughout the Island but seems to be nowhere common.

Witch hazel liniment, used for muscle aches and bruises and as a wash for eye inflammations, is derived from the bark and leaves of the plant. This wonderful shrub is also firmly entrenched in folklore, as forked witch hazel branches were, and presumably still are, a preferred wood in the manufacture of divining rods. When used correctly, these rods have the uncanny ability to locate the presence of water. Correct usage, however, is clearly an art and not a science.

A mist sinks at dawn,
form is lost to abstraction,
all is mystery.

Where To See Witch Hazel

As mentioned above witch hazel is not common in any one location, since it does not seem to grow in colonies or dense stands on Long Island.

Prosser's Cathedral Pines County Nature Preserve — on the east side of County Route 21 about half a mile north of the Longwood Road intersection. A very large multi-stemmed plant grows in an open area on the north, or to the left, of the dirt entrance road.

Montauk County Park and Montauk State Park — witch hazel is scattered throughout the rich woods situated on the south side of Big Reed Pond and throughout the western portion of the state property.

St. John's Preserve — situated behind (south of) the Cold Spring Harbor Fish Hatchery. Several plants are scattered along the nature trail.

LARGE CRANBERRY. (Robert T. McGrath)

CHAPTER TWENTY-THREE

They Called It Red Gold: Cranberries

Most Long Islanders know the important role potatoes have played in Long Island's agricultural past and are aware of the emerging importance of viticulture, embodied in the sixteen or so vineyards that have become established on the North and South Forks. Few, however, realize the past significance of the cranberry industry on the Island. In fact, during the latter half of the nineteenth century, Long Island was the third largest cranberry producing area in the country. Unfortunately, today there are no commercial cranberry bogs left in operation. The last one, the Davis Bog in Manorville, harvested its final crop in the fall of 1975.

The large cranberry, a member of the blueberry family (see Chapter 7 for other blueberry family members), is a vinelike shrub that can reach a foot in length and often trails along the ground. It is a plant native to Long Island and is found along the sandy edges of bogs throughout Canada and the northern United States. Its scientific species name, *macrocarpon*, means large fruit, a fact that was not lost on the revolutionary war soldier who first attempted to cultivate it. In contrast, its close cousin, the small cranberry, found in similar boggy habitats, has not been widely cultivated.

The most commonly offered explanation for how the cranberry got its name is that to the pilgrims, the flower blossom looked like the head of a crane (presumably the sandhill crane, which might have frequented the cranberry's wetland haunts) and so they named it craneberry. Through the years the "e" was dropped.

Low-lying, flat areas with sandy, acidic soil and a supply of acidic water are necessary requirements for the cultivation of cranberries. Since these conditions were abundant on Long Island, the region was ideal habitat for cranberries. It was in the Pine Barrens, or more precisely along the Peconic River which flows through the Pine Barrens, where these conditions were most abundant, and it was along the river and within its headwater systems that the most successful cranberry bogs were located.

Creating a cranberry bog meant much more than just planting a few vines and waiting for them to produce berries. The native vegetation, in most cases shrubby, swamp growth, had to be cleared down to the peat. Several inches of sand to serve as the bed for the vines had to be laid. Sand was also required for construction of the earthen dike and weir system necessary to control water levels. Not surprisingly, the sand most often used was that which was closest. At Cranberry Bog County Nature Preserve in Riverhead, a borrow pit, which once contained the sand required to construct the dike creating Swezey's Pond, can easily be seen along the nature trail which circumscribes the pond.

The vines were then planted in rows about a foot apart. Once established, it took an average vine about five years to begin to produce cranberries (talk about a slow return on your investment!). During this time an activity known as "sanding the bogs" was conducted every third year. A coating of sand was laid on the vines to stimulate their growth while suppressing unwanted weeds. The benefit of sanding was inadvertently learned after a bog on Cape Cod was covered with sand (the result of a hurricane). The vines produced more berries than ever the following summer.

A series of channels, both dissecting the bog and running around the perimeter, were also dug. These channels were necessary to insure that all parts of the bog would receive adequate amounts of water.

Harvesting was hard work too. Cranberries ripen in late summer and are ready for harvest from late September through early to mid-October. Harvesting was initially done by hand within set lines (early photographs of bogs resembled a course set for the 100 yard dash) to insure efficient harvest of the crop. Later, wooden hand scoops were used which had tines that were a little bit narrower than the diameter of a small cranberry. The scoops greatly speeded the harvest. It also caused men to replace women in harvesting, as the two-handled scoop was too heavy for most women to use. Finally, mechanical pickers were employed which were more efficient yet.

Once harvested, the cranberries had to pass the "bounce test." Early on in cranberry cultivation it was discovered that a healthy cranberry bounces easily while a sickly one does not. All cranberries were routed through a bouncer possessing a minimum of seven small hurdles which the berries had to make it over. (The Suffolk County Parks Department has a bouncer and other harvesting equipment that was donated to it when the County acquired the Davis Bog as part of R.C. Murphy County Park in 1986.)

After harvest, the bogs were flooded for the winter to a depth that prevented the vines from freezing or being desiccated by winter winds. In the spring, they were drained to allow the vines to receive the sun's rays and to permit pollination of the flowers. Any threat of frost though, and the bogs would be flooded again in short order. At the Davis Bog section of R.C. Murphy County Park, you can still see the remains of the pump house that once housed a diesel engine. The engine was attached to a large belt, which in turn was connected to a paddle wheel. When the engine was turned on, the wheel could move large amounts of water into the bog rather quickly.

There were about a dozen major bogs on Long Island and probably another dozen or two smaller ones. The first was in Bayport in 1870 where today, at Camp Edey Girl Scout camp or the adjacent San Soucci County Nature Preserve, the sandy dikes can still be seen. Word quickly spread to the east where major bog operations began. The Woodhull Bog south of Riverhead, in what is now Cranberry Bog County Nature Preserve, became one of the biggest. Created in 1885 by the Woodhull brothers of Riverhead, the cranberry vines were planted the next year. In 1889 the first harvest was achieved: ten bushels. The next year was better with some ninety bushels harvested. Things then picked up; 500 bushels were taken by 1891, and by 1892 more than 21,000 bushels, at two dollars each, made it to market. For the next forty years, the cranberry business was as bright as the color of the cranberry itself. No wonder the crop was called red gold.

But the Long Island growers always lagged behind those in New Jersey and Cape Cod where thousands of acres of bogs produced the overwhelming majority of berries. Moreover, there were not enough Long Island growers to warrant the establishment of a processing factory. One by one, the bogs went out of business until, by World War II, only a handful remained.

Then the bottom fell out. A few days before Thanksgiving in 1959, the federal Food and Drug Administration announced that amino triazole, a weed killer commonly used on cranberries, caused cancer. Few people bought cranberries that or the following year. Eventually only one bog remained: the Davis Bog in Manorville. In 1976, this too expired when the owner stated that due to years of neglect, it would take $1.5 million and seven years to restore the bogs. Long Island was out of the cranberry business.

But there is an important footnote to the story. A new cranberry bog is currently being developed in Cutchogue on the North Fork. Perhaps we will have red gold once again.

Where To See Cranberries

While wild cranberry vines can be found in suitable habitat throughout eastern Long Island, the best place to see them and pick a few is at one of the former commercial bogs. These include:

The Davis Bog in **Robert Cushman Murphy County Park** — Manorville. While some sections of the bog system are in an advanced state of neglect, other sections still have good numbers of vines. The bogs run for nearly a mile from Swan Pond south, across River Road, nearly to the main channel of the Peconic River.

Cranberry Bog County Nature Preserve — south of the Riverhead traffic circle on County Route 51. The site of the former Woodhull Bog, you can see the earthen dam, excavated area and small patches of cranberries.

To see cranberries growing naturally visit the Fox and Sandy Pond section of **R.C. Murphy County Park,** located off Line Road (about three-quarters of a mile west of the Davis Bog).

Napeague State Park — in Napeague, where cranberries grow naturally in narrow, linear bogs.

Fire Island National Seashore — cranberries and other wetland plants are often found in low-lying swale areas between the primary and secondary dunes along the stretch of the seashore.

Key Times

Cranberries in flower — late June through early July
Ripe cranberries — mid-September through mid-October

CHAPTER TWENTY-FOUR

WHITE-TAILED DEER, BUCK. (Robert T. McGrath)

Bambi in Suburbia

THE WHITE-TAILED DEER

In an open grassland in Westhampton that I was combing in search of grassland birds such as meadowlarks and grasshopper sparrows, I happened upon a fawn that was lying still, nose to tail, in a slight depression. The only movement she made was with her eyes which carefully tracked me, and her nostrils which gently sniffed my unfamiliar scent. Equally still, I relished the sight of the beautifully speckled animal for a minute or two before moving on.

Some might be surprised to learn that this experience occurred recently. As Long Island's natural places have become increasingly fragmented and developed, many species have not been able to adapt and have declined or disappeared. Reasons for this decline, such as increased predation, parasitism and loss of suitable feeding habitat, have also driven the white-tailed deer, the largest mammal found on the Island, from much of its former range. But unlike many other species, deer continue to thrive, where given half a chance. The relative success of the white-tail in adapting to modern Long Island, however, is viewed in a variety of contrasting ways by the people who now share their habitat.

Native Americans and European colonialists viewed the deer as meat on the hoof, and many contemporary enthusiasts concur. Others are shocked by such an attitude, and instead see the animal as the essence of natural innocence, gentleness and beauty. Still others classify deer as vermin, due to their taste for exotic and expensive shrubbery, or as a vector for disease. Along with its alternative host, the white-footed mouse, the white-tailed deer serves as a host for the spirochete which carries Lyme disease.

Deer feed most actively toward dusk and dawn, often in open, exposed areas. They feed quickly, consuming large quantities of vegetation before moving back into protective cover to "chew their cud" for much of the evening and day. Like cows, deer have the ability to regurgitate their food and rechew it, thereby breaking it down more completely. They do this in the safety of woodlands adjacent to their feeding areas.

The sexes remain apart for most of the year. Bucks congregate in groups of three to five, and does travel in larger groups that include yearlings and current-year fawns. They come together in the fall to mate (usually in October) after which the fertilized female rejoins her original group. The male, on the other hand, feels no family responsibility and continues his search for receptive females.

Fawns are born in late May to early June. For the first few weeks of their life they remain detached from their mothers, hiding in vegetation and only meeting with her to nurse. After about a month the fawn travels with the mother, and they rejoin the female group in late summer. The fawns lose their distinctive spots when they molt their summer coat in the fall.

In the absence of the animal itself, it is a delight to play animal detective by searching for signs of its presence. The white-tailed deer leaves more evidence than most. As with people, deer prefer to move through fields and woodlands on already established trails, thereby avoiding the need to bushwhack. These trails or runs meander through field and forest and often are barely perceptible, requiring you to look down their length for a distance to be sure that they are, in fact, trails. Rubbed-off hair can sometimes be found on the branches of shrubs which line the sides of the runs.

Deer will not hesitate to use existing trails and dirt roads as well, and it is on these that their footprints can frequently be seen. Deer prints are quite distinctive, and it is highly unlikely you will confuse them with those of any other native mammal. Each print consists of a pair of crescent-shaped imprints that curve inward and are thick in the back and narrow toward the front. Bucks have the largest prints, about two and a half inches long, females the next largest and fawns, as you might expect, the smallest, at about one and a quarter inches. Occasionally, on soft ground such as mud or snow, you can make out two small, imprinted dots that trail the crescents. These are the impressions of the dew claws, small toes that are situated above the main foot.

Also along trails you may see another sign of deer: scat. Deer scat consists of two dozen or so oval to cylindrical-shaped pellets dropped together. The only other animal's sign with which they might be confused is that of the cottontail rabbit, but rabbit pellets are round instead of oval.

If you come across a small tree or sapling where the bark has been rubbed smooth or entirely off, you are witness to yet another sign of white-tailed deer (they seem to especially like young red cedars). Bucks begin to grow new antlers each spring, and they are mature by late summer to early fall. A velvety layer, filled with blood vessels, covers the antlers and provides nourishment while they grow. Once the growing is complete, the velvet (which is another occasionally seen sign of deer) begins to unravel. The buck uses saplings to assist in removing the velvet strands. While most rubbings do not injure the tree severely, occasionally the buck rubs so hard it rips off several inches off bark, which may ultimately prove fatal to the tree.

Other signs of deer include deer scrapes and beds, but these as well as shed antlers are less often seen. There is good reason for the lack of antlers lying scattered about: they are rich in nutrients and are quickly gnawed by mice, chipmunks and squirrels.

Where To See The White-tailed Deer

While it is possible, and in some places probable, that you will see deer in various woodlands from central Suffolk County east, there are several locations where the chance of seeing them borders on near certainty. Morning and late afternoon are the best times to see deer. These locations are:

Connetquot River State Park Preserve — in Great River/Oakdale. There is a resident deer herd within the park. Deer are most reliably seen between the main entrance and the fish hatchery.

Hecksher State Park — in East Islip. This park too has a resident deer herd. Individuals are almost certain to be seen in a drive around the park's main loop road in late afternoon to early evening.

Navy Property — in Calverton. The several-thousand-acre federal facility here is home to much more than airplane hangers and fighter planes. A large deer herd is found within the property and individuals can be seen from the perimeter feeding at several points within the fenced-in enclosure. Looking into the property along the north side of Grumman Boulevard (also known as Swan Pond River Road) where it is intersected by Line Road is especially productive.

The Long Island Expressway and **Sunrise Highway.** Deer can often be seen feeding along the shoulders of the more easterly stretches of these highways.

Fire Island — deer can be commonly seen along the length of this barrier island from **Robert Moses State Park** eastward, through the **Fire Island National Seashore,** to **Smith Point County Park.** The thickets around the Fire Island Lighthouse are usually a good place to see deer.

CHAPTER TWENTY-FIVE

DOUBLE-CRESTED CORMORANT. (Marc Oliveri)

Cormorants

Due to their mobility, birds illustrate the flux of nature more than any other group of animals. While some birds have declined or disappeared from Long Island, others have increased, or have recently become breeders for the first time.

Such is the case with the double-crested cormorant, or "DC squared" as it is called by some birders. An ornithological account from the last century would not have included the bird as a breeder in New York. In fact, a 1942 handbook on the birds in the vicinity of New York City reported the double-crested cormorant as a migrant with only occasional records of summer and winter visitors.

This began to change in 1945 when a breeding colony became established on a small island in eastern Lake Ontario. By the late 1970s the bird reached Long Island, and today there are two breeding colonies, involving several hundred birds each, situated on Gardiner's Island and on a series of small islands north of Fisher's Island. Groups of cormorants, resting on offshore rocks or fishing net poles with wings outstretched, or swimming about in the surf with their bills slightly upraised, have become common sights along Long Island's coastline.

The wingspread or eagle-winged posture of cormorants is a response to wet feathers. Although you might expect a bird that dives for fish to have evolved waterproof feathers (as many diving birds have done), such is not the case with cormorants. If submerged for long periods, their outer feathers become waterlogged, diminishing the bird's ability to fly or pursue fish underwater. As a result, cormorants spend a lot of time "airing out" their wings.

Double-crested cormorants owe their name to the pair of dark feather tufts adult birds grow during the breeding season. These tufts are not easy to see, though, and the observer should look instead for the bright orange throat pouch and dark iridescent plumage as diagnostic field marks of the species. First-year birds are much lighter in color, especially on the throat and stomach.

The birds eat fish almost exclusively, and this dietary preference has brought them trouble. A favorite fishing spot is within the pound nets seen throughout the coastal waters surrounding eastern Long Island. Fisherman have been known to dispatch those caught swimming around in them.

Cormorants breed both on the ground and in trees, constructing roughly made nests from sticks and branches. Leaves and seaweed are used as lining material. They feed their young regurgitated, slightly digested fish, at first by dripping the mixture from their bill tip, and later by opening the bill and allowing the chicks to dip in, as if feeding from a soup pot. This protein-rich mixture causes the young to mature quickly, and they are fully developed in a little more than three weeks.

The great cormorant, the double-crested's larger cousin, is a regular winter visitor but does not reproduce here; its breeding range is much further north, extending south only to Nova Scotia.

Where To See Cormorants

Double-crested cormorants can be seen in Long Island coastal waters in dozens of locations. They are common on Long Island Sound, Peconic and Flanders Bays, the south shore bays, and off Montauk Point. They can also be seen in many coastal ponds.

They are particularly common on **Shinnecock Bay** in and around the inlet or roosting on adjacent sandbars. They are reliably seen on **Tobay** or **Guggenheim Pond** at the Town of Oyster Bay's **Tobay** or **John F. Kennedy Sanctuary,** as well as at the tip of **Orient Point County Park** and on the **Orient Point Lighthouse Island** located in Plum Gut.

Great cormorants are not reliable in any one location, but your best bet may be in the waters surrounding Montauk Point.

Key Times

Double-crested cormorants can be seen during the spring, summer and fall months, but are particularly common in autumn because of the addition of offspring from the recently concluded breeding season. This is a good time to study the plumage differences between adult and immature birds.

Great cormorants can first be seen in late autumn beginning around mid-November; they are rarely seen after early March.

WOOLLY BEAR CATERPILLARS. (C. F. Nichols)

CHAPTER TWENTY-SIX

Woolly Bears

AUTUMN'S CATERPILLARS

Given their generally larger size, brighter colors and flight capabilities, it is usually the adult insect (the butterfly, moth or beetle) that is the most well known. Woolly bear caterpillars are one of the few insects where the opposite is true: the larvae is better known than the adult. While many people immediately recognize this distinctive black- and orange-banded caterpillar, not one in a hundred is able to identify the adult tiger moth into which it transforms.

From mid-October to mid-November (and sometimes into early December if the weather is mild) the caterpillars seem to be everywhere as they search for a log or slab of bark under which to overwinter. They are about one and one-half inches long and are covered with scores of one-quarter-inch-long bristles, giving them the appearance of small bottle brushes. Though bristly, the caterpillars are harmless and will routinely curl into a tight ball in your hand if picked up.

The middle bristles are orange and the bristles at either end are black. The relative length of caterpillar cloaked in each color is the stuff of legend: if the central orange band is narrow, the winter will be cold, while a wide orange band forecasts a mild winter. Although the relationship between the severity of winter and band width provides the amateur meteorologist with ample opportunities for prognostication, scientific studies of the phenomenon have been inconclusive at best.

Woolly bears belong to the family *Arctiidae*, the tiger moths, so named because of the bright, bold color patterns found on some of the species. The most commonly seen woolly bear on Long Island is the banded woolly bear or the Isabella tiger moth. The forewings are yellow and the hind wings are salmon. Both wings are speckled with black dots.

The typically thick bodies are imbued with a variety of colors including rust, orange, yellow and tan and are variously dotted and striped.

When crossing open areas such as a path, caterpillars can race along at speeds of up to five feet per minute (about one-eighteenth of a mile per hour). At such a rate it takes a caterpillar about five minutes to make it across an average neighborhood road and twenty minutes to cross the Long Island Expressway. This period of time is clearly lethal and highlights the deadly impact of heavily traveled roads on slow-moving animals. As Long Island continues to develop and natural areas become increasingly fragmented, smaller woodland areas undoubtedly will become devoid of many of the slower ground-moving species.

Where To See Woolly Bears

Because woolly bears feed on plant species that are common throughout Long Island, such as plantain, various grasses and trees like hickory, woolly bear caterpillars are common. They can be seen in virtually every major park in New York City and Nassau and Suffolk Counties.

Key Times

The caterpillars are most active, and therefore most easily seen, during the fall, after they have finished their late summer feeding and are searching for a place to hibernate. They are especially active from mid-October through mid-November. If the weather is mild, and the caterpillars are active into December, will all the caterpillars have wide central bands?

Winter

BLACK-CAPPED CHICKADEE. (Maria T. Weisenberg)

OLDSQUAW. (Marc Oliveri)

CHAPTER TWENTY-SEVEN

Bobbing Birds, Swimming Seals

WILDLIFE AT MONTAUK POINT

In a world that is becoming more and more dominated by humans, there are fewer places where large concentrations of wildlife can still be viewed. One welcome exception to this trend is at the Island's eastern tip, Montauk Point, where thousands of water birds congregate each winter, drawn by the abundant mussel beds and other food items flanking the shore.

Sea ducks often dominate the scene. One can watch eiders, scoters, mergansers, oldsquaw and goldeneye as they bob in the ocean waves, or fly back and forth in long skeins. Whirling overhead, walking along the rocky shore, or resting in an orderly, evenly-spaced fashion on top of the pavilion, are the ubiquitous gull species: great black-backed, herring and ring-billed, as well as the rarer winter gulls, the glaucous and the Iceland.

Common and **red-throated loons** are often interspersed in the waterfowl flocks, cloaked in their winter plumage (drab when compared to their handsome summer garb). As late winter blends into early spring, common loons occasionally are heard yodeling. The sound seems displaced on the marine waters of Montauk Point, especially if you have been fortunate enough to have heard their summer breeding choruses on freshwater lakes throughout the northern United States and Canada. **Horned grebes** are here too, but can be easily overlooked since they are small and spend much of their time submerged, searching for food.

Both the **double-crested** and the **great cormorant** overwinter at Montauk. They are easy to pick out from all the other floating and swimming birds. Look for the dark-colored "duck" that swims with its hook-tipped bill slightly elevated, as if it were snubbing the other birds.

Sharing the waves with the loons, grebes, sea ducks and "snooty" cormorants are the true marine birds generally referred to as **alcids:** murres, razorbills and the occasional guillemot or dovekie. These are birds that nest in fantastic numbers on cliff sides throughout the Canadian arctic and maritime provinces. The gannet, a large bird that is a member of the booby family, shares the precipitous terrain of the alcids' nesting grounds and joins them off Montauk in winter. Long Island is one of the southernmost points these northern species reach, as the bulk of the population overwinters in the north Atlantic. Nonetheless, respectable numbers turn up at Montauk and other areas along Long Island's coast each year. Flocks of razorbills, with their massive, laterally compressed bills, are the most reliably seen of the alcids.

Two species of eiders (from whose nests the eider down of pillow and parka fame is collected) occur regularly at the point. They are the **common** and the **king eider,** with the common living up to its name as the more abundant. Flocks occasionally reach into the hundreds. The adult drakes are easily distinguished and are among the most beautiful ducks in the world. Immature males and females, however, are a different story, and sometimes the birder must become resigned to identifying a duck as an eider and just leave it at that.

Three species of scoters make the Point a hum of winter activity. On some days these ducks are ceaseless in their movements, and a person watching birds for several hours will never be out of sight of groups of flying or diving scoters. Their abundance was made clear to me on a winter trip in February, 1993. I had set up my birding scope to scan a flock of eiders several hundred yards from shore, but before doing that I focused on the coastline of Block Island, shimmering in the distance. In doing so, I realized that a steady stream of scoters, at a rate of at least ten a second, were flying past. The flight movement continued unabated, and after stopping the count forty minutes later, rather bleary eyed, I estimated that approximately 25,000 ducks had flown past. As large a number as this is, it pales in comparison to a flock of nearly 200,000 scoters that were reported from the Point during the winter of 1930.

The **white-winged scoter** is generally the most common species in the waters surrounding the point. It has distinctive, easily recognizable white wing patches (hence the name) with a small, white half-moon found beneath the eye. The **surf scoter** is the most colorful of the group with a pretty black, white and orange bill and two large white spots on the front and back of the head. The **black scoter,** not surprisingly, is the darkest of the three, but is not difficult to spot with the bright, orange-yellow knob on its nose.

Red-breasted mergansers are also quite common in the waters off Montauk Point. The species is easy to identify, even in relatively poor light, due to its distinctive shaggy-headed profile. All three mergansers (see Chapter 28 for a discussion of the common and hooded mergansers) have serrated bills which assist them in holding onto their diet of slippery fish. Unlike the previously mentioned species, the red-breasted merganser breeds on Long Island, albeit rarely. Its nests are known from the south shore and the east end

The **oldsquaw,** wonderfully named and beautifully marked, is less frequently seen at Montauk than some of the other waterfowl species, although it is a regular here and a visit is likely to produce several birds. It has a graceful, long-plumed tail, and distinctive black-and-white winter plumage. The winter plumage looks like a photographic negative of the summer plumage with white in the winter where black occurs in the summer and vice versa. The oldsquaw is one of the deepest-diving ducks and has been recorded at depths of nearly 200 feet. They can remain submerged for more than two minutes.

The handsome **goldeneye,** accurately named because of its doll-like, gold-colored eye, is easy to separate from other duck species because of its prominent, round, white cheek patch and dark green head. The only bird it is likely to be confused with is its cousin the **Barrow's goldeneye** (its cheek patch is crescent-shaped and its head is dark purple). Large flocks of a hundred or more birds are sometimes seen off Montauk's coast.

A most spectacular bird, the **gannet,** is here listed last, but it is certainly not least. The gannet is a goose-sized bird with a six-foot wingspan, and while immature birds are sooty brown with white speckling, adults are snow white with jet black wing tips. They capture fish by taking dramatic plunges from a hundred feet or more, behavior reminiscent of the osprey. To watch a flock of several hundred adult gannets, diving on a school of fish, sending up plumes of spray as they strike the water, is a sight one can often experience at Montauk, and is one of the most thrilling wildlife experiences available on Long Island.

Birds are not the only animal class that frequents the near-shore waters at Montauk. The class *Mammalia* is represented by the large-eyed **harbor seal,** a common winter guest. In some winters a dozen or more seals can be spotted. They are especially regular along the north side of the Point where they can be seen swimming about in the waves. A perch on the rocks at the base of the lighthouse is a fine vantage point to see seals, since they come close to shore due to the deep water. I will long remember a harbor seal here which broke the surface just below me with a large flounder wriggling in its mouth.

When resting, harbor seals often "haul out" on offshore rocks, with those dozing on low rocks being routinely nudged by the waves. Harbor seals also can be found throughout Peconic Bay and the south shore bays and are regularly seen at Shinnecock and Moriches Inlets.

GANNET. (From *The Water Birds of North America,* by Baird, Brewer, Ridgway)

Where to See Wildlife at Montauk Point

To maximize your chances of seeing the birds mentioned in this chapter, it is important to bring binoculars and find a good vantage point so that you are looking down on the water. By doing so you get a better angle to see floating birds and seals. Good vantage points include the patio next to the pavilion, the rocks positioned at the base of the lighthouse (be careful since they can be slippery) and a hill that is midway between the pavilion and the lighthouse. The hill is reached by a trail that starts at the parking lot (near the main entrance) and winds along the pavilion to the water. After coming out on the shore, turn right and you will see a denuded hill in front of you (made barren by tens of thousands of footsteps) which you should climb to enjoy the view.

To view resting seals, walk along the northern beach about a mile and one-half west. You will see a jumble of several dozen rocks jutting out into the water perpendicular to the shore. Harbor seals routinely haul out on these rocks. PLEASE DO NOT GET ANY CLOSER THAN ABOUT 200 YARDS, OR THE SEALS WILL BECOME DISTURBED. SINCE WINTER IS THEIR MOST STRESSFUL TIME OF YEAR, THEY NEED TO REST. DO NOT DISTURB OR HARASS THEM.

Key Times

The birds mentioned usually arrive at Montauk by the middle of November and linger through mid- to late March. The same time frame holds for seals.

CHAPTER TWENTY-EIGHT

REDHEAD. (Marc Oliveri)

Bottoms Up!

WINTER DUCKS

The onset of winter brings chilly blasts of arctic air that are not entirely welcome, but birders know that the arrival of more cordial visitors — flocks of waterfowl — is now imminent. They look forward to this time when they can leisurely scan a pond with binoculars or birding scope to observe the multi-specied rafts.

The freshwater ponds and lakes which dot Long Island, and the sheltered, brackish-water bays and harbors which fringe it, combine to make one of the best locations in the United States to watch native species of waterfowl. In early December, before some of the less hardy ducks have headed south, but after others have arrived from more northerly locations, as many as three dozen species can be tallied in a single day. Few other regions of the country can match this diversity (see Chapters 27 and 31 for a discussion of other species).

Despite the propensity of the "ugly duckling" to turn up in children's stories and colloquial conversation, there are no ugly ducks in the wild. Drakes range from handsome, as in the gadwall and black duck, to pretty, as with the ring-necked or ruddy duck, to downright beautiful, as with the hooded merganser and wood duck. The trademark wingpatch, or speculum, brightly colored in most species, adds to the beauty of the group. With the notable exception of the monomorphic black duck, most ducks are sexually dimorphic, meaning that males (drakes) and females (hens) look different. In all cases the hens are less colorful, and exhibit a more subtle beauty. In contrast, the sexes of geese and swans look the same.

The male **mallard** with its emerald green head is probably the most well-known species of waterfowl. Found on most freshwater ponds and lakes throughout Long Island, it is our most common breeding duck. The white collar, chestnut brown chest, grayish sides, and purple blue wingpatch also help to identify the male mallard. The female is mottled brown with the same purple blue speculum.

In the early part of this century the New York Department of Conservation released several thousand pen-raised mallards. This release, coupled with escapees from collections and estates, produced the duck we know today which is, for the most part, a semi-domesticated bird. The picture becomes more complicated by the fact the mallard interbreeds with Pekin and Rouen ducks, common domesticated forms, as well as many of the wild dabbling duck group of which it is a member. As a result, a group of mallards swimming about at the local feeding pond may well be made up of several hybrid forms.

Interbreeding between the mallard and the black duck is of great concern. This threat was first recognized about thirty years ago, and is caused by alterations in habitat that have brought the species together, particularly in late winter when the birds begin pairing up for the upcoming nesting season. Mallard-black duck hybrids are now common and there is strong concern among wildlife managers that the black duck, as a distinct species, may disappear altogether.

As its name suggests, the **black duck** is a dark-colored bird; dark brown with a paler colored head, a beautiful purple-colored speculum, white underwing linings that flash when the bird takes flight and bright orange feet. Black ducks are among the wariest of ducks, often being the first to flush when disturbed.

The **gadwall** is the plainest of all. Looking akin to a business man in a gray flannel suit, the male is mostly gray with a black rump and brown head. The only bit of color is the white wing patch which becomes quite evident when the duck takes flight. The female is mottled light brown and is similar to a female mallard.

The **pintail** is unmistakable. The drake pintail has a graceful pin-like tail, a chocolate brown head with a white stripe running up its side, white neck and breast, and gray sides. It is one of the most attractive species to grace our ponds and lakes. The female can be told from other female ducks by her sleekness, dark bill and pointed tail.

The **American widgeon** is a common overwintering duck on Long Island. It is also known as the baldpate, bald in this case meaning white (the same derivation as the white-headed bald eagle) and pate meaning forehead. The American widgeon is tannish in color and has a green crescent behind the eye. It also has an emerald green speculum and a large white wing patch on the forewing.

Its European cousin, the **European widgeon,** is a regular cold weather visitor to Long Island with reports of half a dozen turning up each winter season. The European drake differs from its American counterpart in that it has a tan-colored forehead, and a rich rusty-colored head. Its body is grayer in appearance and has an identical wing pattern of green and white. Ornithologists suspect that a small breeding population of this duck now exists in the western hemisphere.

Two species of teal are present on Long Island during the winter, although the **blue-winged teal,** with its distinctive, white, crescent-shaped face patch, usually departs by early December for warmer climes. (It migrates the farthest of any duck, typically overwintering in the northern part of South America.) The **green-winged teal,** one of our smallest ducks, is a beautiful combination of green and rich brown. Its speculum is, as its name indicates, a brilliant, emerald green.

The **shoveler** wins the most unusual duck award. Both sexes have a disproportionately large, spatulate bill which is adapted for straining aquatic life. The shoveler's wings are as beautiful as its bill is odd with a powder blue front patch and a bright green speculum.

"Ol' white cheek," the **ruddy duck,** is a common waterfowl species on Long Island. In breeding season the male is rich ruddy brown in color with a bright white cheek patch, black cap and a pretty, chalky blue bill. The ruddy has a pert, upturned tail that serves as a handy field mark. In winter the duck turns a drab brown and its bill turns a dullish gray, but its white cheek patch is still evident.

The name of the **ring-necked duck** is misleading. Even in the best light its orange-colored collar is but faintly visible. The ring on its bill however is quite striking, and along with the bright white vertical line that separates the flank from the breast, serves as a valuable long-distance field mark. It should be called the "ring-billed" duck instead.

We have two red-headed ducks that overwinter on Long Island: the **redhead** and **canvasback.** These are difficult for many beginning birders to tell apart since they both have a pretty, brick red head, black breast and grayish sides. The profile of the head is useful in separating these two species: the redhead has a more rounded head and hence a higher forehead than the canvasback. They also can be told apart based on their bill: the canvasback's is black, while the redhead's is a pretty black, white and powder blue. Both species are more common in the western United States.

The two most stunning ducks to grace our freshwater ponds in the winter are the wood duck and the hooded merganser. Any description of the multi-hued, male **wood duck** fails to do the bird justice, but we will try. It has a crested, green head with white lines in the crest, a white throat with two white fingers that jut into the green head, a bright orange bill and eye, chestnut brown chest (often spotted) separated from straw-colored sides by two vertical white and black lines and a bluish brown iridescent back. Wood ducks usually depart for their wintering habitat in the southeastern United States by early December.

The **hooded merganser** (once called by the wonderfully colloquial names of hairy-head, the whistler or the water pheasant) has a distinctive oriental aspect to it. It has a large, puffy head made even larger when it puffs up its crest to reveal its unmistakable white crest patch. The duck is an appealing combination of white, black and tan. It has a small, serrated black bill

The wood duck and hooded merganser have something in common besides their good looks: they both nest in tree hollows or other nesting cavities. Because of this habit, wildlife managers often put up nesting boxes in suitable wetland habitats, and there have even been reports of the two ducks sharing the same box. Both species have been recorded as Long Island breeders, although the wood duck is much more common.

Two other species of mergansers occur on Long Island: the ubiquitous red-breasted on salt water (see Chapter 27) and the **common merganser** (a bit of a misnomer since it is less common than the red-breasted). The male common merganser has a bright green head, a bright orange red bill and a white body which is noticeable for quite some distance when seen on large lakes such as Lake Ronkonkoma.

All species of mergansers have bills with hooked tips and serrated edges. The edges act as teeth to help these fish-eating specialists hold onto their slippery prey. Since teeth are comparatively heavy, birds long ago "evolved away" their teeth as an adaptation for flight. In place of teeth, some birds, such as mergansers, evolved serrated edges that fulfill the same function.

While mergansers feed primarily on fish, many species of waterfowl, particularly those frequenting freshwater ponds, consume plant life. These plants generally take three forms: small floating plants such as duckweed; floating emergents, plants that float on the surface, but are rooted in the bottom of the pond, such as pondweed and water lilies; and submergents, plants that are rooted in the shallow pond bottom, but do not reach the surface, such as coontail or water milfoil.

It is when feeding on submergent plants that ducks attain their comical "bottoms up" posture with their posterior parts pointing into the air, a display accented by the pintail with the "pin" pointing toward the tall blue sky.

The **Canada goose** is a common (some say too common because of the stunning volume of effluvia left by grazing flocks) visitor to freshwater ponds and lakes throughout the Island. Due to a change in their behavior wrought by human changes to the local environment — particularly our love for lush lawns and golf courses — Canada geese are now frequent nesters and therefore summer residents. These resident birds are joined in the colder months by migratory geese which have bred across northern Canada.

While several of the species described above occur in both fresh- and saltwater environments, such as the black duck, a few other ducks prefer the brackish, sheltered waters found in the bays and harbors that form the Island's wonderfully tortuous coastline. These include the greater scaup (its close relatives, the lesser scaup and ring-necked duck, usually inhabit freshwater), bufflehead and red-breasted merganser (for a discussion on the red-breasted merganser and other saltwater ducks see Chapter 27). Members of the goose family, such as the brant also prefer coastal waters.

The **bufflehead,** one of the smallest ducks, is an easy waterfowl species to identify. The male has a striking, white, U-shaped patch on a dark-colored head, and the female can be identified by her small oval cheek patch. Bufflehead overwinter in small groups of up to thirty birds.

With the nesting season behind them, males of many duck species "turn cryptic." They molt their beautiful breeding plumages and sport nondescript "eclipse" plumages (their radiant beauty eclipsed by the more mottled appearance). Males are flightless during the eclipse, since they molt their flight feathers along with their body contour feathers. During this time, lasting anywhere from several weeks to a few months, the males closely resemble females, making it difficult, if not impossible, to distinguish the sexes.

If, upon a trip to your favorite pond, all the beautiful male mallards seem to have taken wing and flown off, remember they cannot take wing, but are right in front of you, eclipsed by ladies' clothes. Ornithologists believe this camouflage cross-dressing evolved as an adaptation to a time when the male birds are vulnerable to predation, just as the female evolved permanently inconspicuous plumage to protect her and her duckling-rearing capabilities.

Buy a Stamp, Protect a Duck

Probably the single most important action a conservation-minded person can undertake is the purchase of a federal duck stamp (officially known as the Migration Bird Hunting and Conservation Stamp). Available annually, the stamp currently costs fifteen dollars, and its purchase is mandatory for anyone wishing to hunt waterfowl.

Why, you might ask, should you spend fifteen dollars if you are more interested in watching birds than shooting them? The simple answer is that the duck stamp is one of the most successful wildlife conservation measures ever enacted. Of the money raised, 99.9 percent goes toward the acquisition of wetlands and other wildlife habitat critical to waterfowl.

Since its inception in 1934, more than $350 million worth of duck stamps have been sold, resulting in the purchase and protection of more than four million acres. Many of the national wildlife refuges so popular to bird watchers have been partially or entirely purchased with duck stamp proceeds.

An added benefit of the duck stamp is that it provides free access to refuges that charge an entrance fee. You can buy a duck stamp at your nearest post office.

Where to See Winter Waterfowl

While almost any freshwater body larger than a puddle is apt to be used by some ducks or geese, the following ponds or lakes have proven over the years to be successful:

Blydenburgh Pond in **Blydenburgh County Park** — good vantage points include the boat rental dock on the south side of the park and the historic grist mill on the north side. Since a trail network parallels most of the pond's shoreline, good views of wintering waterfowl are to be had if you are willing to walk for them.

Lake Ronkonkoma — this large, glacial kettlehole lake often has large rafts of ducks. The County Park properties in the northwest and eastern sections of the shoreline, as well as other vantage points along Portion Road are worthwhile spots to scan for waterfowl. Despite some interesting legends, the lake is not bottomless, or connected to the ocean by a mysterious subterranean connection. Its quite normal bottom is, however, about ninety feet deep.

Canaan Lake — in North Patchogue. Parking along Webb Avenue at the southern end of the lake can provide good views of the entire lake and its waterfowl visitors.

Note: A *recommended day trip for viewing winter waterfowl involves driving along the south shore on* Montauk Highway *(also known as* Merrick Road, South Country Road, *etc.) from* Merrick *to* Eastport. *A few dozen southward-flowing streams such as* Massapequa Creek, Orowoc Creek, Brown's River, *and* Swan

River were dammed when Montauk Highway was constructed, creating many small to medium-sized ponds on the north side of the road. Driving from pond to pond, most of which are easily accessible, can be a particularly efficient way to get to know the waterfowl species that overwinter on Long Island. Consult a local atlas to plan the best route.

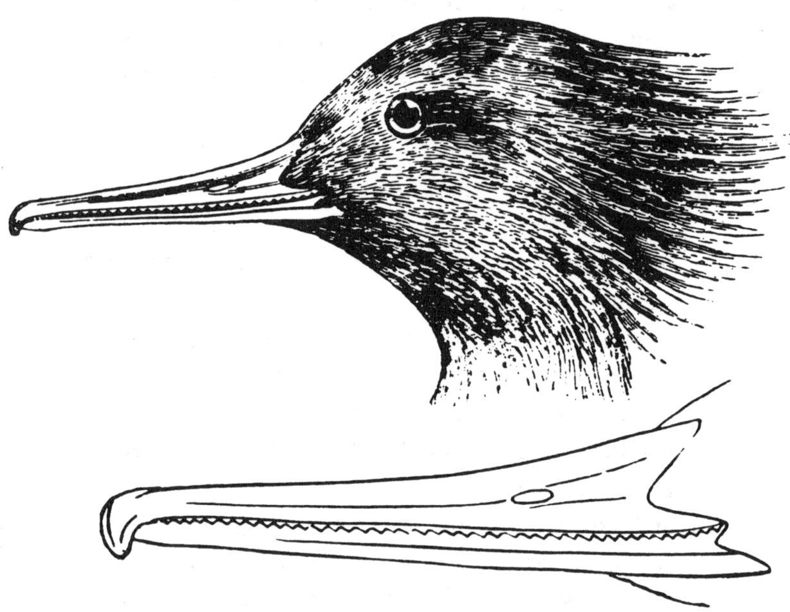

RED-BREASTED MERGANSER. *(From The Water Birds of North America,* by Baird, Brewer, Ridgway)

CHAPTER TWENTY-NINE

AMERICAN CROW. (Marc Oliveri)

Trees Filled with Crows

I remember an early summer day fifteen years ago when I climbed to near the top of a black oak to have a look at a crow's nest. My anticipation mounted as I drew closer to the rim of the nest. It was securely set between several sturdy branches that formed the top of the tree, about fifty feet above the ground. In the middle of the nest were four beautiful, blue eggs, scrawled with dark maroon markings. As the tree swayed gently in the breeze, I thought it was natural for the eggs to be blue, having been struck by the color of the sky.

Even if most people have not scaled a tall tree to look in on one of their nests, crows join the ubiquitous house sparrow and starling as a regular part of most Long Islanders' daily experience. Hardly a winter day goes by that a commuter on the Northern State Parkway, or the Long Island Expressway, does not see a flock of crows flying overhead, or a few individual birds searching for food along the roadside. In fact, there is probably nowhere outdoors on Long Island where a person could stand for a day and not see at least one of these most common birds.

The crow (or more accurately the **American** or **common Crow**) is one of the more common nesting birds on Long Island. It was confirmed as a possible breeder in ninety-three percent of more than 5,000 censused blocks during a statewide survey conducted in the mid-1980s.

The nest often has a bulky look to it due to the use of relatively large branches as construction material. But like most songbirds (yes, the crow is considered a songbird) the inner cup of the nest is lined with finer material such as shreds of grape vine, bark, leaves, fur and fine roots. Crows will nest in a variety of trees including oak, beech, maple and evergreen species such as hemlock and pine. While four to five eggs are most often laid, as few as three and as many as eight are possible. The eggs hatch in about eighteen days.

During the spring, crows pair up to form mating couples and are widely dispersed throughout the countryside in established territories. As nesting season ends, however, and summer folds into fall, crows begin to change their behavior. They abandon their breeding territories to congregate in large flocks. By mid-winter the flocks are well established, and the most obviously impressive aspect of crow life becomes evident: their massive nightly roosts.

One historical roost on Long Island held more than 50,000 birds, although the ones existing today are in the 6,000 to 9,000 bird range. Even so, to stand on the periphery of a woodland as this many crows fly in on the dusk of winter's day is not a scene soon to be forgotten. The birds seem to use "pre-roost" staging areas where several hundred crows from a given area will congregate before moving on to the main roost.

The **fish crow,** a close cousin of the common crow, is also a Long Island native. As its name suggests, the fish crow is most common along the coastline where they can often be found foraging. Unlike the common crow, which has a widespread nesting distribution throughout the state, the fish crow is restricted to Long Island and the Hudson River valley.

The fish crow is very difficult to distinguish from the common crow by sight, although it is slightly smaller. It is easily identified by its call, though, which is a higher-pitched "*caa, caa*" that sounds like a common crow with a bad head cold.

Crows belong to the family *Corvidae* which includes ravens, magpies and jays. The common blue jay is the only other corvid found on

Long Island, but the northern raven and gray jay are other New York State family members. The raven nests in the Catskill and Adirondack Mountains, while the gray jay, as a nesting bird, is restricted to the Adirondacks.

Corvids have long been known to be among the most intelligent of all birds. Although not as fluent as parrots, crows are known to speak, and the captive crow at the Quogue Wildlife Refuge reminds you of your location by occasionally verbalizing "*Quo- Quo- Quogue*."

They also were among the first birds known to use tools. Ravens may toss rocks when defending their nest, and crows are known to drop food items such as nuts and clams onto hard surfaces, such as parking lots, in order to break the shell and get at the meat. More interestingly, crows have been seen adding rocks to a pool of water in an attempt to raise the level of the water so they could more easily drink from it. Also, in a remarkable example of problem solving, crows seem to understand sequences. In an experiment, a researcher placed a row of bottle caps in front of a crow. Food was placed under the first cap, which the crow found by trial and error. The food was then put under the second cap, which when overturned rewarded the crow. It was then placed under the third cap. After a short while the crow knew to dispense with random flipping of caps and to focus on the cap adjacent to the one which previously had hidden the food.

Crows are omnivorous, meaning they are not restricted in their eating habits, but will consume many things both animal and vegetable. For example, they perform a great public service by removing, free of charge, thousands of road-killed animals scattered on Long Island roadways. As with blue jays, they are known to eat nestling birds and bird eggs and have been implicated in the decline of many songbirds (see Chapter 8).

Where To See Winter Roosts of Common Crows

There are several crows roosts that are easily visited. One of the largest is the one situated in the woods on the southeast corner of Smithtown Boulevard and Mayfair Road in Nesconset. The crows use the woods that are partly within a park owned by the Town of Smithtown and partly on adjacent, privately owned parcels which are slated to be developed.

Why not try to find other winter roosts by watching the direction crows fly in during late afternoon?

Crow with stick in beak,
confirms it's nest building time,
flies strongly toward pine.

CHAPTER THIRTY

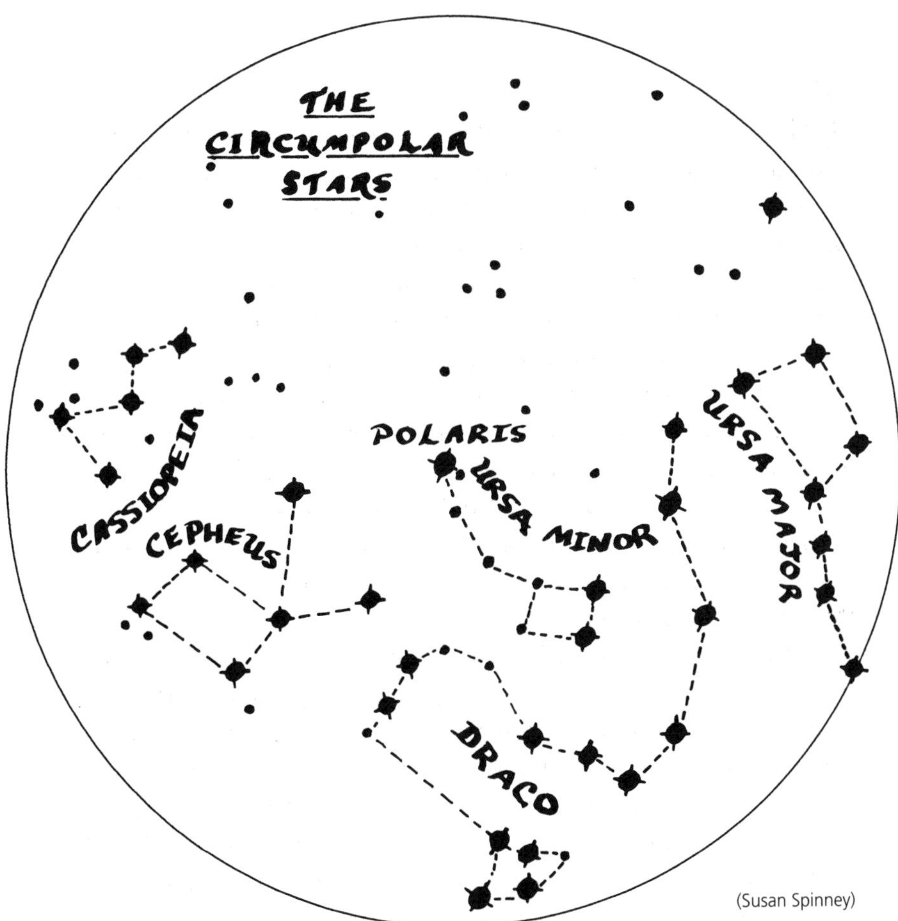

(Susan Spinney)

The Winter Sky

"There's nothing like astronomy to pull the stuff out of man. His stupid dreams, or red rooster importance, let him count the STAR SWIRLS."

— Robinson Jeffers

Each celestial season reveals its own special gifts, whether it be constellations, meteor showers or planetary alignments. Winter, however, gives us the clearest skies and the 2,000 or so stars that the average person can see are brighter due to less atmospheric moisture. So, in spite of the cold, it is a favorite time for hardy nature lovers to leave the warm confines of their homes and turn their eyes upward to stargaze.

Consider the **Big Dipper,** or as it is also known, the plough or the wagon. It is probably the most well-known astronomical feature of our night sky, and although it is not deemed a constellation by itself, being a part of Ursa Major, the Great Bear, it serves as a convenient starting point for learning the night sky. People's general familiarity with the Big Dipper stems in part from the fact that at our latitude (about 42 degrees north) it never sets, a trait it shares with other constellations known as the circumpolar constellations.

The Big Dipper can be broken into the "handle" which has three stars (the tail of the bear) and the "pot" containing four stars. The two stars of the pot farthest from the handle, Merak and Dubhe, are the famous pointer stars. If you follow a line formed by the pointers northward, about five times the distance that separates them, you should be able to locate **Polaris,** the Pole or North Star. All of the stars of the Big Dipper except Dubhe, the pointer star closest to the North Star, and Alkaid, the star at the end of the handle, are moving in the same direction. This means that in about 40,000 years (for those who think long-term) you will have to find a new means of finding Polaris.

Many people are disappointed when they first see the North Star, expecting it to be the brightest star in the heavens. Its brightness, or more formally its magnitude, places it in the top third of the pack, but it appears dim for a star of such fame. The North Star is always at true north (actually about one degree off), and from our vantage point on earth, appears to be at the center of the night sky with all the other constellations revolving around it. If you are lost in the woods or disoriented on the highway, the North Star can help set you straight: as you face it, south is always to your back, east to your right and west to your left.

Several stars in the Big Dipper are interesting in their own right. **Mizar,** for example, the star forming the bend in the handle has another fainter star next to it called **Alcor.** The name reportedly means the "near one," a reference to its closeness to Mizar. In reality, Alcor is not that close to Mizar, it just appears that way from our vantage point. It has been reported that Native Americans used these stars as a means for testing visual acuity. If a warrior could see Alcor, his vision was sufficiently sharp to allow him to join hunting parties. They referred to Mizar and Alcor as the "horse and rider" or the "squaw with the papoose on her back."

Mizar is famous for another reason. It was one of the earliest binary (double) star systems discovered, meaning that it has a companion, much closer than Alcor, to which it is gravitationally connected, each revolving around the same imaginary pole. Binary stars were first discovered when astronomers realized that the light emitted by certain stars seems to fluctuate in brightness. They learned that when one of the stars slid behind the other, the total amount of light diminished and then increased again once the two ceased to overlap.

The North Star is part of the **Little Dipper,** a less conspicuous constellation that looks like a miniature of the Big Dipper. It fits with the Big Dipper a little bit like the Chinese yin-yang symbol. The brightest star in the Little Dipper is Kochab, and it along with its neighboring star are sometimes referred to as the guardians of the pole.

If you continue on the line established by the pointer stars of the Big Dipper through Polaris you will come to the constellation of **Cepheus** the King. It is a disappointing constellation with mostly faint stars. With a little imagination though, you can make out a king with a square-shaped head wearing a triangular crown.

A more recognizable constellation is the king's companion, **Cassiopeia** the Queen. She can be found by extending a line beginning with the star that forms the base of the handle in the Big Dipper (called Megrez) through Polaris. This will bring you to the Queen. Actually, she does not look anything like a queen. Rather, depending on the time of day or season, she looks very much like an M or a W, with the right side of the M, or the left side of the W, being slightly flattened.

If you were to tie a line to the star farthest to the right in the W (or farthest to the left in the M) and let it drop, it would pass by one of the most interesting features in the night sky, and the most distant object that the unaided human eye can see in the universe: the **Andromeda Galaxy.** It will appear as a fuzzy patch and can best be seen when looked at indirectly. The galaxy is approximately one and a half million light years away from earth, meaning the light we see when we view the galaxy actually left it one and a half million years ago.

Imagine the Big Dipper is a pot holding water. If the bottom sprung a leak, it would spill onto the back of **Leo** the Lion, one of the few constellations that actually looks like its description. (Actually, the way I remember the location of Leo is to make believe the pot of the Big Dipper is filled with milk which is leaking onto the back of a cat that, of course, likes to drink it.) The most prominent feature of the constellation is the "sickle," a large backwards question mark that forms the head of the animal. The Leonid meteor showers, occurring around November 16, emanate from an area just inside the sickle. **Regulus,** one of the brighter stars in the northern hemisphere, forms the paw of the Lion's right leg.

Back we go again to the Big Dipper. This time, follow a long line extending from Megrez through Dubhe and you will arrive at the dominant winter constellation — **Orion** the Hunter. His right arm is erect holding a club, his left arm is holding a shield (to ward off onrushing Taurus the Bull), and he has three bright stars in a tight row that make up his belt. A sword hangs from his belt, and here the famous Orion Nebula is located.

Orion has two of the brighter stars in our sky. **Betelgeuse** (pronounced *beetle juice*) forms the right shoulder of the hunter. It has a reddish tint to it and is known as a red giant. It is estimated to be 400 times larger than our sun and is more than 3,000 times as bright. **Rigel,** forming the hunter's left foot, is a mere thirty times as large as our sun and is a brilliant bluish white.

If you follow a line from the belt stars in a direction away from Orion's shield, you will arrive at **Sirius,** the brightest star in our sky. It is part of a rather nondescript constellation called **Canis Major,** or the Big Dog.

After finding Sirius follow, in a more or less straight line, through Betelgeuse and on for the same distance again, and you will arrive at a wonderful skymark — the **Pleiades.** Also known as the Seven Sisters, the Pleiades look like a tiny Big Dipper and sometimes are mistaken for it. The Pleiades are in the constellation of **Taurus** the Bull.

Return to the Big Dipper one last time. This time we follow the arc of the handle away from the Big Dipper and arrive at a bright orange-colored star called Arcturus (a convenient way to remember: arc to Arcturus). Arcturus is part of a constellation known as **Bootes** the Herdsman, but to me it looks more like an ice cream cone with some of the ice cream licked away. Next to the ice cream cone is the **Corona Borealis,** or Northern Crown. While it looks a bit like a tiara, it looks more like a scoop of ice cream that has fallen off the adjacent Bootes.

On a particularly clear night you may make out a fuzzy band of light that arcs across the sky. It passes through Cassiopeia and Cepheus and the club of Orion. This band of light is our own **Milky Way** Galaxy and the light we see is the collective luminescence of the 100 billion or so stars that make up the galaxy (our sun being one of them). The Milky Way is shaped like a pinwheel, and our solar system (the sun and the nine planets) is located out on one of the arms of the pinwheel. We see a band of light because we are looking at the galaxy in cross-section.

Where To See The Night Sky

Diminishment of wildlife and loss of open space are not the only casualties of development. The night sky is affected too. The more Long Island develops, the more lights from shopping centers, homes and highways there are to compete with the natural light from the stars. The Milky Way is often a casualty. Still, on clear nights you should be able to find locations that enable you to enjoy the night sky.

An excellent place is along the **South Shore Barrier Beach.** Not only do you not have to worry about competing light in the southerly direction, due to the Atlantic ocean, but you have an unobstructed view to the horizon in all four directions.

If you cannot get to the beach, viewing the night sky from the athletic field of a neighboring school can be productive. The point is to try to find a location where you have as unobstructed a view to the horizon as possible, and where it is dark enough to see the stars.

A number of worthwhile guides and sky charts are available to help you learn to navigate the skies above Long Island. If you do bring these navigational aids with you in the field, a flashlight will be necessary to read the chart. Place red cellophane paper over the flashlight lens. You will still be able to read the chart, and your eyes will not take as long to adjust to the darkness when you refocus on the stars.

CHAPTER THIRTY-ONE

SNOWY OWL. (Marc Oliveri)

Feathered Denizens from the North

Many people think of the winter season on Long Island as a time when bird life has fled to warmer climes, leaving the Island's wild places to a few, hardy survivors. In the case of dozens of species of migratory songbirds this perception is true. Few realize, however, that during this same time the Island's bird life is supplemented by an influx of several species from more northerly regions. These birds range from the four-inch pine siskin to the rough-legged hawk with its five-foot wingspan; from the ubiquitous white-throated sparrow to the rare gyrfalcon.

Some of these birds, referred to as *irruptive species*, move south not to leave the bitter cold behind (being superbly insulated they can tolerate the cold), but to find a reliable food supply. If there is an adequate food supply, many irruptive species will not leave their northern haunts regardless of how cold it is. These species, including several owls, hawks and winter finches, are not reliable on Long Island every winter. Other winter visitors turn up routinely here each winter.

The **snowy owl** is probably the most famous example of an irruptive species. When the owl's food supply of various species of lemmings and voles drops (most of these species have a multi-year cycle which swings from abundance to scarcity), the birds are forced to move south. This is particularly true for the immature "hatchyear" birds (born earlier that year) that lack hunting experience.

With its striking white plumage and bright yellow eyes, this winter visitor from the north is one of the most impressive birds seen on Long Island, or, for that matter, anywhere in the world. One does not soon forget a view of a snowy owl sitting on the crest of a sand dune staring intently back with its piercing yellow eyes.

The number of snowy owls reported each winter on the Island varies from as few as three or four to as many as a dozen. Most of the birds are immature, identified by the numerous, black, crescent-shaped fleck marks scattered throughout the bird's plumage. Adult females are lighter but still have some flecking, and adult males, the rarest of the three, are virtually snow-white. These owls prefer open, treeless areas that are similar to its tundra breeding grounds.

The **gyrfalcon** and **rough-legged hawk,** raptors from the far north, routinely appear on Long Island during the winter, although in fewer numbers than the snowy owl. The gyrfalcon comes in several color phases or morphs — white, gray and black (or dark). Like the snowy owl it has a fondness for open, windswept places.

The rough-legged hawk, so named because of the abundance of feathers that cover its legs, also exists in color morphs: a light and a dark phase. It displays a characteristic hovering flight when hunting over fields.

A number of **finches** are also classified as irruptive. These include the common redpoll, pine siskin, red and white-winged crossbills and the evening grosbeak. Of these species, the evening grosbeak is the only one that will routinely feed at a backyard feeding station, and lucky is the homeowner who hosts a flock of these colorful black, white and yellow birds.

The **yellow-rumped warbler,** so named because of its diagnostic lemon yellow rump patch, is one of the more common winter visitors along barrier beaches. The splash of yellow it displays when flitting about provides an eye-catching contrast to the subdued tones of the winter coastal landscape. The yellow-rumped is common here because its primary winter food source, the waxy bayberry of bayberry candle fame, flourishes in coastal areas. This berry-eating habit is unusual among insect-eating warblers and is why the yellow-rumped can overwinter on Long Island and throughout the Northeast, while other warblers cannot. It is also a common spring and fall migrant, so keep it in mind when exploring the places described in Chapters 8 and 20.

The **purple sandpiper** and the **harlequin duck,** one a shorebird, the other a waterfowl species, share a fondness for the same type of overwintering habitat: rocky jetties and breakwaters. The harlequin duck is unmistakable with its rust-colored side, purple body and odd-shaped patches and dots. It prefers rough water, just the kind you find adjacent to jetties. Purple sandpipers play it a bit safer, preferring to stay on the rocks of the jetties where they scurry about in search of food brought in by the overwashing waves.

This chapter would be incomplete if we failed to mention the **white-throated sparrow** which breeds across the lower half of Canada and the northern United States. The white-throated is currently an abundant winter visitor, but with established breeding populations as close as the Catskills, it may become a confirmed breeder on Long Island in the near future. Almost any bramble or thicket will have overwintering sparrows which betray their presence with a penetrating "*tseet! tseet!*" call.

Where To See Feathered Winter Visitors

The snowy owl prefers open country and is most commonly reported from the south shore barrier beach. Owls are reliably reported from **Jamaica Bay Wildlife Refuge, Floyd Bennett Field, Jones Beach** and **Robert Moses State Parks, Cedar** and **Overlook Beaches** in Babylon, and **Smith Point County Park.** Snowy owls are also reported from **Shinnecock East** and **West County Parks** (the parks straddling the **Shinnecock Canal**) and from **Shinnecock West County Park** west along Dune Road for approximately three miles. The gyrfalcon and rough-legged hawk also prefer open treeless areas and can be seen along the barrier beach. The rough-legged also can be seen hunting on occasion in large open fields somewhat inland from the coast.

The winter finches are highly irregular in their movements and are difficult to find with predictability. Crossbills and pine siskins prefer the cones of evergreen trees, so groves of these trees can sometimes prove fruitful. Evening grosbeaks often appear at backyard bird feeding stations, while redpolls prefer overgrown fields and can be found along their edges. The yellow-rumped warbler can be seen at **Jones Beach** and **Robert Moses State Parks,** the **Tobay Sanctuary** east of Jones Beach and other public parks on the barrier beaches and along the south shore mainland.

The purple sandpiper and harlequin duck almost always associate with rock jetties. The jetties along each side of the inlets of the south shore bays such as **Jones Inlet** (particularly the Point Lookout side), **Moriches Inlet,** and **Shinnecock Inlet** are a good bet to see these species. White-throated sparrows are prevalent in winter and can be seen in overgrown fields and thickets in virtually every park mentioned in the book.

Key times

These winter visitors arrive by mid-November and depart usually by mid- to late March.

White-throated sparrows,
perching in bramble of rose,
chirp in winter cold.

BLACK-CAPPED CHICKADEE. (Robert T. McGrath)

CHAPTER THIRTY-TWO
The Black-Capped Chickadee
A BIRD IN THE HAND

Like many parks and preserves, I had heard of the Morton National Wildlife Refuge, situated in Noyac on the north side of the South Fork, long before first visiting it. It sounded enchanting with its nesting ospreys and easy-to-see deer. The peninsula itself juts north a mile and a half into Little Peconic Bay, providing some of the most beautiful views of land and water the East End has to offer.

It was a little three-inch bird, the black-capped chickadee, that captured my imagination, however, and served as the prime motivation for my wanting to visit the refuge. The resident flock here is special because, thanks to a previous property owner who tamed these inquisitive birds, the chickadees feed out of your hand. If you are especially lucky, a tufted titmouse or white-breasted nuthatch may alight as well.

During the colder months, from early November through late March, it is almost certain that a bird will alight in your hand if it is stocked with unhusked sunflower seeds (make sure they are unsalted; salted seeds can be harmful). You will hear the soft flutter of wings, feel tiny feet grasping a finger, and if your chickadee is a finicky sort, it may shuffle about on your palm in search of the finest seed of all. Sometimes two birds will pick among the seeds together, but usually only one bird feeds at a time. It will issue its aggressive "gargle" call to deter other chickadees from landing.

With seed in mouth, the chickadee flies to a nearby protected perch where it hammers open the seed with its bill, gaining leverage by wedging it tightly between its feet and a branch. If sated, the bird will cache the seed by jamming it under a curled piece of bark, in a small crevice or perhaps a knothole. Occasionally, chickadees will store seeds in the ground, and there are records of them caching seeds in drain-pipes and gutters, in backyard swing sets, and even under shingles. Research indicates that black-capped chickadees have excellent short-term memories, so relocating the cached food is not a problem.

Spend a few minutes around a flock of black-capped chickadees, and it becomes apparent how they received their name. The bird is unmistakable among songbirds, with its handsome and prominent black cap and bib framing a white cheek patch, and it will not be long before an individual gives off its distinctive *"chick-a-dee"* call.

The upper back of a chickadee is mousy gray, sometimes suffused with buff. The sides are buffy, and along the edge of the wings and the tail are streaks of white. The bill is black, as is the eye, although the eye is concealed by the black cap.

The black-capped chickadee is one of the most common songbirds in the eastern United States. It breeds in a variety of woodland types, ranging from orchards, pine plantations, suburban woodlots, oak-pine forests and open deciduous forests. In New York it breeds in every part of the state except perhaps a few of the boroughs of New York City.

The chickadee is a cavity nester, and if it does not use a chamber previously excavated, perhaps by a woodpecker, it will make its own by chipping away wood from a rotten limb or stub. Most nests are within eight to fifteen feet of the ground. The cavity is lined with plant fibers, feathers, rootlets, hair and bits of dried moss.

Unlike birds that lay their eggs in open situations, and therefore have evolved eggshells that are heavily pigmented to aid in their concealment, cavity-nesting chickadees' eggs are white with flecks of reddish brown concentrated toward the wider end of the egg. They are incubated only by the female and hatch in two weeks; the male contributes by bringing his mate food. The helpless, blind chicks develop rapidly and fledge in about sixteen days.

As colder weather takes hold, the mated pair hooks up with other chickadees to form flocks of ten or more birds. During the winter, chickadees will mix with other species, including white- and red-breasted nuthatches, its close cousin the tufted titmouse, ruby- and golden-crowned kinglets, brown creepers and downy woodpeckers. Observing these roving flocks is one of the joys of winter birding.

Surviving the cold of winter is a particular challenge for a warm-blooded animal as small as a chickadee. Given its diminutive size, its surface-to-area ratio is much higher than it is for you or me, and were it not for its body feathers, which do a remarkable job of insulating the bird, it would lose heat at a rapid rate.

The bird has developed two interesting ways to reduce heat loss; one behavioral and the other physiological. On particularly cold nights, chickadees will seek out a cavity in which to roost. By heating the air space within the cavity, which reduces the temperature difference between the bird and the air around it, the chickadee is able to reduce its loss of body heat. This reduces the amount of energy the bird must expend during a period of the day when it obviously is unable to feed. There even are records of chickadees roosting overnight in a hollow chamber they've made in the snow.

Perhaps more remarkable than this behavioral adaptation to surviving cold is the physiological one: chickadees are able to drop their body temperature ten to twelve degrees Centigrade during the night. Doing so reduces the amount of energy consumed. This technique, called regulated hypothermia, results in energy savings as great as twenty-five percent, a factor that might prove critical during very cold weather or when food is especially scarce. Other bird species are also known to have the ability to regulate their body temperature.

Where To See Black-Capped Chickadees

Since black-capped chickadees are common, year-round residents on Long Island, they can be seen at all seasons and in many locations. They are regular visitors to backyard bird feeding stations. However, a trip to the **Morton National Wildlife Refuge** in Noyac will enable you and your children to experience the magic of feeding chickadees by hand.

Unhusked, UNSALTED (as stated above salt can be lethal to birds) sunflower seeds are best and can be easily found in the pet supply aisle of your neighborhood supermarket. Do not buy the bird seed mix that contains millet and other seeds. Chickadees prefer sunflower seeds and will come to your hand more readily than to your neighbor's if yours is filled soley with a pile of this gourmet item.

Key Times

The best time for hand-feeding black-capped chickadees is during the winter months when natural foods have become scarce. A visit between November 1 and March 1 should provide you and your family with an enjoyable day.

APPENDIX ONE

Natural History and Conservation Organizations

There are quite a few organizations based on Long Island that are involved in trying to protect wild places and open spaces and/or provide environmental education programs. Following is a list of some of those. Any and all of them would greatly appreciate your financial and volunteer support.

American Littoral Society
New York Chapter
28 West 9th Rd.
Broad Channel, NY 11963
(718) 634-6467

Audubon Society, Four Harbors
Box 126
East Setauket, NY 11733

Audubon Society, Great South Bay
P.O. Box 916
Bayport, NY 11705

Audubon Society, Huntington
P.O. Box 735
Huntington, NY 11743

Audubon Society, Lyman Langdon
P.O. Box 763
Port Washington, NY 11050

Audubon Society, Moriches Bay
P.O. Box 802
Center Moriches, NY 11934

Audubon Society, South Shore
P.O. Box 31
Freeport, NY 11520

Group for the South Fork
117 Main Street
P.O. Box 569
Bridgehampton, NY 11932
(516) 537-1400

Long Island Botanical Society
P.O. Box 905
Levittown, NY 11756

Long Island Pine Barrens Society
P.O. Box 429
Manorville, NY 11949
(516) 369-3300

The Nature Conservancy
Long Island Chapter
250 Lawrence Hill Road
Cold Spring Harbor, NY 11724
(516) 367-3225

North Fork Environmental Council
Route 25 at Love Lane
P.O. Box 799
Mattituck, NY 11952
(516) 298-8880

Okeanos Ocean Research Foundation
P.O. Box 776
278 East Montauk Highway
Hampton Bays, NY 11946
(516) 728-4522

Open Space Council
P.O. Box 275
Brookhaven, NY 11719

Sierra Club, Long Island Chapter
P.O. Box 210
Syosset, NY 11791

South Fork Natural History Society
P.O. Box Nature
Amagansett, NY 11930

APPENDIX TWO

A Long Island Naturalist's Bookshelf

One of the clear advantages to nature study today is the wide variety of high-quality field guides available on virtually every natural subject area ranging from trees to stars to seashells. These books are often the most popular titles in the nature section of your local bookstore.

Foremost among those guides are the Peterson Field Guide Series, named for the originator and author of the first guide in the series — Roger Tory Peterson, who wrote *A Field Guide to the Birds* (1934). More than three dozen guides in that series assist naturalists in studying all aspects of the natural world including trees, ferns, wildflowers, reptiles and amphibians, mammals, butterflies, insects, edible plants and stars and planets.

Capitalizing on the success of the Peterson Field Guides, other field guide series and individual guides have found their way onto the shelves of your local bookstore. The Golden Field Guide series contains several guides on such topics as birds, trees and amphibians. They too are worthwhile additions to your collection.

The Stokes Nature Guide series takes a slightly different approach. Less a catalog aimed primarily at identification, these guides contain more in-depth descriptions of various subject areas. *The Guide to Amphibians and Reptiles*, for example, covers only thirty-two species but goes into detail about each species' life history, affording the reader a better understanding and appreciation of the animal. They are excellent companions to the more traditional identification guides.

Two other highly recommended guides are *Newcomb's Wildflower Guide* and *The National Geographic Society's Guide to Birds of North America*. The illustrations in the Newcomb's guide are exceptional, and it contains an easy-to-use locator key for quick identification of wildflowers. The NGS guide has illustrations of certain bird groups that are more complete than the Peterson or Golden bird guides.

In addition to the above-mentioned general guides on nature, there are a number of worthwhile books and articles that deal specifically with the natural history of Long Island. While the following list is by no means exhaustive, many of the more well-known books and papers are included.

Books

Andrle, Robert F., and Janet R. Carroll. 1988. *The Atlas of Breeding Birds in New York State.* Ithaca: Cornell University Press.

Brodo, Irwin M. 1968.*The Lichens of Long Island, New York: A Vegetational and Floristic Analysis.* Albany: New York State Museum and Science Service .

Bull, John. 1964. *Birds of the New York Area.* New York: Harper & Row.

———. 1974. *Birds of New York State.* Ithaca: Cornell University Press.

Connor, Paul. 1971. *The Mammals of Long Island,* New York. Albany: New York State Museum and Science Service.

Johnson, Ann F. 1985. A *Guide to the Plant Communities of the Napeague Dunes, Long Island, New York.*

Murphy, Robert C. 1962, 1991. *Fish-Shape Paumonok: Nature and Man on Long Island.* Great Falls, VA: Waterline Books.

Peters, George H. 1973. *The Trees of Long Island.* Oyster Bay: The Long Island Horticultural Society.

Puleston, Dennis. 1992. A *Nature Journal.* New York: W.W. Norton & Company.

Shapiro, Arthur M. 1974. *Butterflies and Skippers of New York State.* Ithaca: Cornell University Agricultural Experiment Station.

Articles

Conard, H. S. 1935. "The plant associations of central Long Island." *Am. Midl. Nat.* 16: 343,481–487.

Cryan, J. F. 1980. "An introduction to the Long Island pine barrens." *The Heath Hen* 1:3–13.

———. 1982. "The Long Island dwarf pine plains: pygmy forests of the pine barrens." *The Heath Hen* 1:3–33.

Ferguson, W. C. 1924. "Contributions to the flora of Long Island, New York." *Bull. Torrey Bot. Club* 51: 177–201.

———. 1925. "Ferns and flowering plants of the Hempstead Plains, Long Island, New York." *Torreya* 25: 109–113.

Fuller, M. L. 1914. "The Geology of Long Island, New York." U.S. *Geol. Surv. Prof. Paper,* No. 82231 p.

Harper, R. M. 1912. "The Hempstead Plains of Long Island." *Torreya* 12:277–287.

Lamont, E. E., J. M. Beitel, and R. E. Zaremba. 1988. "Current status of orchids on Long Island, New York." *Bull. Torrey Bot. Club* 115: 113–121.

Latham, R. A. 1940. "Distribution of wild orchids on Long Island." *Long Island Forum* 3: 103–107.

McGrath, R. T. and J. L. Turner. 1985. "Some orchids of the Long Island pine barrens." *The Heath Hen* 2:32–39.

Stalter R., E. E. Lamont and J. Northup. 1986. "Vegetation of Fire Island, New York." *Bull. Torrey Bot. Club* 113:298–306.

Zaremba, R. E. and E .E. Lamont. 1993. "The status of the Coastal Plain Pondshore community in New York." *Bull. Torrey Bot. Club* 120: 180–187.

APPENDIX THREE
Scientific Names

As illustrated by trailing arbutus in the Chapter 7 (Blueberries), scientific or Latin names can be fun to learn and often provide useful information about the life history of the plant or animal in question.

Following is a list of the common and scientific names of *The Other Island's* plants and animals in order of their appearance.

Chapter 1
Spring Wildflowers

skunk cabbage—*Symplocarpus foetidus*
marsh marigold—*Caltha palustris*
red-winged blackbird—*Agelaius phoeniceus*
wood anemone—*Anemone quinquefolia*
flowering dogwood—*Cornus florida*
dwarf ginseng—*Panax trifolius*
spring beauty—*Claytonia caroliana*
yellow trout lily—*Erythronium americanum*
red trillium—*Trillium erectum*
nodding trillium—*Trillium cernuum*
painted trillium—*Trillium undulatum*

Chapter 2
Tigers in the Night

tiger salamander—*Ambystoma tigrinum*
spotted salamander—*Ambystoma maculatum*
blue-spotted salamander—*Ambystoma laterale*
marbled salamander—*Ambystoma opacum*
northern two-lined salamander—*Eurycea bislineata*
four-toed salamander—*Hemidactylium scutatum*
red-backed salamander—*Plethedon cinereus*
red-spotted newt—*Notophthalmus viridescens*
wood frog—*Rana sylvatica*
spring peeper—*Hyla crucifer*
Fowler's toad—*Bufo woodhousei*
leopard frog—*Rana pipiens*
pickerel frog—*Rana palustris*
gray treefrog—*Hyla versicolor*
green frog—*Rana clamitans*
bullfrog—*Rana catesbyiana*
spadefoot toad—*Scaphiopus holbrooki*

Chapter 3
Plovers, Terns and Skimmers

piping plover—*Charadrius melodius*
little (least) tern—*Sterna albifrons*
common tern—*Sterna hirundo*
roseate tern—*Sterna dougalli*
black skimmer—*Rynchops nigra*

Chapter 4
The Flight of the Woodcock

American woodcock—*Philohela minor*

Chapter 5
The Osprey's Return

osprey—*Pandion haliaetus*
bald eagle—*Haliaeetus leucocephalus*
peregrine falcon—*Falco peregrinus*
brown pelican—*Pelicanus occidentalis*

Chapter 6
The Return of the Alewife

alewife—*Alosa pseudoharengus*
American shad—*Alosa sapidissima*
shadbush—*Amelanchier canadensis*

Chapter 7
Blueberries

trailing arbutus—*Epigaea repens*
bearberry—*Arctostaphylos uva-ursi*
wintergreen—*Gaultheria procumbens*
striped wintergreen—*Chimaphila maculata*
blueberry—*Vaccinium spp.*
huckleberry—*Gaylussacia spp.*
mountain laurel—*Kalmia latifolia*
sheep laurel—*Kalmia angustifolia*
fetterbush—*Leucothoe racemosa*
maleberry—*Lyonia ligustrina*
swamp azalea—*Rhododendron viscosum*
leatherleaf—*Chamaedaphne calyculata*

Chapter 8
Songbird Migration

Bachman's warbler—*Vermivora bachmanii*
yellow warbler—*Dendroica petechia*
yellowthroat—*Geothlypis trichas*
ovenbird—*Seiurus aurocapillus*
pine warbler—*Dendroica pinus*
prairie warbler—*Dendroica discolor*
scarlet tanager—*Piranga olivacaea*
rose-breasted grosbeak—*Pheucticus ludovicianus*
northern oriole—*Icterus galbula*
indigo bunting–*Passerina cyanea*
cedar waxwing—*Bombycilla cedrorum*
eastern bluebird—*Sialia sialis*
wood thrush—*Hylocichla mustelina*
robin—*Turdus migratorius*
eastern phoebe—*Sayornis phoebe*
wood pewee—*Contopus virens*
hermit thrush—*Catharus guttatus*
black-billed cuckoo—*Coccyzus erythropthalmus*
eastern kingbird—*Tyrannus tyrannus*
bobolink—*Dolichonyx oryzivorus*
common nighthawk—*Chordeiles minor*
American redstart—*Setophaga ruticilla*
whip-poor-will—*Caprimulgus vociferus*
least flycatcher—*Empidonax minimus*

veery—*Cathurus fuscescens*
magnolia warbler—*Dendroica magnolia*
blackpoll warbler—*Dendroica striata*
brown-headed cowbird—*Molothrus ater*

Chapter 9
Fire in the Long Island Forest

jack pine—*Pinus banksiana*
pitch pine—*Pinus rigida*
scrub oak—*Quercus ilicifolia*
dwarf chestnut oak—*Quercus prinoides*
black oak—*Quercus velutina*
scarlet oak—*Quercus coccinea*
white oak—*Quercus alba*
red oak—*Quercus rubra*
sassafras—*Sassafras albidum*

Chapter 10
Long Island's Prairie

bird's-foot violet—*Viola pedata*
wild indigo—*Baptisia tinctoria*
American goat's-rue—*Tephrosia virginiana*
blue toadflax—*Linaria candensis*
dogbane—*Apocynum androsaemifolium*
colicroot—*Aletris farinosa*
sandplain gerardia—*Agalinus acuta*
little bluestem—*Schizachyrium scoparium*
big bluestem—*Andropogon gerardii*
Indian grass—*Sorghastrum nutans*

Chapter 11
The Prickly Pear

beachgrass—*Amophila breviligulata*
dusty miller—*Artemisia stellariana*
clotbur—*Xanthium echinatum*
prickly pear cactus—*Opuntia humifusa*

Chapter 12
Orchids

pink lady's slipper—*Cypripedium acaule*
rose pogonia—*Pogonia ophioglossoides*
calopogon—*Calopogon tuberosus*
white-fringed orchid—*Platanthera blephariglottis*
yellow-fringed orchid—*Platanthera ciliaris*
purple-fringed orchid—*Platanthera psycodes*
crested-fringed orchid—*Platanthera cristata*
ragged-fringed orchid—*Platanthera lacera*
northern wood orchis—*Platanthera clavellata*
downy rattlesnake plantain—*Goodyera pubescens*
ladies' tresses—*Spiranthes sp.*
whorled pogonia—*Isotria verticillata*
small whorled pogonia—*Isotria medeoloides*
cranefly orchid—*Tipularia discolor*

Chapter 13

Dead Man's Fingers

Indian pipe–*Monotropa uinflora*
pinesap—*Monotropa hypopithys*
beechdrops—*Epifagus virginiana*
squawroot—*Conopholis americana*

Chapter 14

"Please Pass the Peas"

blue lupine—*Lupinus perennis*
black locust—*Robinia psedoacacia*
bird's-foot trefoil—*Lotus corniculata*
everlasting pea—*Lathyrus latifolius*
red clover—*Trifolium pratense*
white clover—*Trifolium repens*
rabbit's-foot clover—*Trifolium arvense*
American goat's rue—*Terphrosia virginiana*
wild indigo—*Baptisia tinctoria*
bush clover—*Lespediza sp.*
vetches—*Vicia sp.*
tick trefoil—*Desmodium sp.*
sweet clover—*Melilotis sp.*

Chapter 15

Two Trees

Atlantic white cedar—*Chamaecyparis thyoides*
sweetbay magnolia—*Magnolia virginiana*
northern white cedar—*Thuja occidentalis*

Chapter 16

Plants that Eat Animals

pitcher plant—*Sarracenia purpurea*
round-leaved sundew—*Drosera rotundifolia*
intermediate-leaved sundew—*Drosera intermedia*
thread-leaved sundew—*Drosera filiformis*
bladderworts—*Utricularia spp.*
Venus fly-trap—*Dionaea muscipula*
quill-leaved arrowhead—*Sagittaria teres*
golden hedge-hyssop—*Gratiola aurea*
mermaid weed—*Proserpinica palustris*
marsh St. Johnswort—*Triadenum virginicum*
rose coreopsis—*Coreopsis rosea*

Chapter 17

The Waters Around Us

finback whale—*Balaenoptera physalus*
minke whale—*Balaenoptera acutorostrata*
humpback whale—*Megaptera novaeangliae*
blue whale—*Balaenoptera musculus*
right whale—*Balaena glacialis*
sperm whale—*Physeter catodon*
harbor porpoise—*Phoecenia phoecena*
common dolphin—*Delphinus delphis*
Atlantic bottle-nosed dolphin—*Tursiops truncatus*
spotted dolphin—*Stenella dubia*
Atlantic white-sided dolphin—*Lagenorhynchus acutus*

striped dolphin—*Stenella caeruleoalba*
Atlantic leatherback turtle—*Dermochelys coriacea*
Wilson's storm petrel—*Oceanites oceanicus*
greater shearwater—*Puffinus gravis*
Cory's shearwater—*Calonectris diomedea*

Chapter 18
Southbound Shorebirds

least sandpiper—*Calidris minutilla*
semipalmated sandpiper—*Calidris pusilla*
western sandpiper—*Calidris mauri*
Baird's sandpiper—*Calidris bairdii*
white-rumped sandpiper—*Calidris fuscicollis*
sanderling—*Calidris alba*
semipalmated plover—*Charadrius semipalmatus*
killdeer—*Charadrius vociferus*
black-bellied plover—*Pluvialis squatarola*
ruddy turnstone—*Arenaria interpres*
lesser yellowlegs—*Tringa flavipes*
greater yellowlegs—*Tringa melanoleuca*
short-billed dowitcher—*Limnodromus griseus*
long-billed dowitcher—*Limnodromus scolopaceus*
Hudsonian godwit—*Limosa haemastica*
whimbrel–*Numenius phaeopus*
marbled godwit—*Limosa fedoa*
American avocet—*Recurvirostra americana*
American oystercatcher—*Haematopus palliatus*
willet—*Catoptrophorus semipalmatus*
buff-breasted sandpiper—*Tryngites subruficollis*
upland sandpiper—*Bartramia longicauda*

Chapter 19
Hawks Above the Dunes

sharp-shinned hawk—*Accipiter striatus*
merlin—*Falco columbarius*
Cooper's hawk—*Accipiter cooperii*
northern harrier—*Circus cyaneus*
American kestrel—*Falco sparverius*
red-tailed hawk—*Buteo jamaicensis*
broad-winged hawk—*Buteo platypterus*

Chapter 20
Other Animals Migratory

northern flicker—*Colaptes auratus*
golden-crowned kinglet—*Regulus satrapa*
tree swallow—*Tachycineta bicolor*
monarch butterfly—*Danaus plexippus*
buckeye—*Precis coenia*
red admiral—*Vanessa atalanta*
painted lady—*Vanessa cardui*
variegated fritillary—*Euptoieta claudia*
green darner dragonfly—*Anax junius*

Chapter 21

Witch Hazel

witch hazel—*Hamamelis virginiana*

Chapter 22

The Buck Moth

buck moth—*Hemileuca maia*
black huckleberry—*Gaylussacia baccata*
white-tailed deer—*Odocoileus virginianus*
polyphemus moth—*Antheraea polyphemus*
cecropia moth—*Platysamia cecropia*
luna moth—*Actias luna*
rufous-sided towhee—*Pipilo erythrophthalmus*
brown thrasher—*Toxostoma rufum*
field sparrow—*Spizella pusilla*

Chapter 23

Cranberries

large cranberry—*Vaccinium macrocarpon*
sandhill crane—*Grus canadensis*

Chapter 24

White-tailed Deer

white-tailed deer—*Odocoileus virginianus*

Chapter 25

Cormorants

double-crested cormorant—*Phalacrocorax auritus*
great cormorant—*Phalacrocorax carbo*

Chapter 26

Woolly Bears

woolly bear (Isabella tiger moth)—*Isia isabella*

Chapter 27

Wildlife at Montauk Point

common loon—*Gavia immer*
red-throated loon—*Gavia stellata*
common murre—*Uria aalge*
thick-billed murre—*Uria lomvia*
razorbill—*Alca torda*
black guillemot—*Cepphus grylle*
dovekie—*Alle alle*
northern gannet—*Sula bassanus*
common eider—*Somateria mollissima*
king eider—*Somateria spectabilis*
white-winged scoter—*Melanitta fusca*
surf scoter—*Melanitta perspicillata*
black scoter—*Melanitta nigra*
red-breasted merganser—*Mergus serrator*
common merganser—*Mergus merganser*
hooded merganser—*Lophodytes cucullatus*
oldsquaw—*Clangula hyemalis*
common goldeneye—*Bucephala clangula*
Barrow's goldeneye—*Bucephala islandica*
harbor seal—*Phoca vitulina*

Chapter 28

Bottoms Up!

wood duck—*Aix sponsa*

mallard—*Anas platyrhynchos*
black duck—*Anas rubripes*
gadwall—*Anas strepera*
American widgeon—*Anas americana*
Eurasian widgeon—*Anas penelope*
pintail—*Anas acuta*
blue-winged teal—*Anas discors*
green-winged teal—*Anas crecca*
shoveler—*Anas clypeata*
ruddy duck—*Oxyura jamaicensis*
ring-necked duck—*Aythya collaris*
redhead—*Aythya americana*
canvasback—*Aythya valisineria*
Canada goose—*Branta canadensis*
brant—*Branta bernicula*
greater scaup—*Aythya marila*
lesser scaup—*Aythya affinis*
bufflehead—*Bucephala albeola*

Chapter 29
Trees filled with Crows

house sparrow—*Passer domesticus*
starling—*Sturna vulgaris*
American crow—*Corvus brachyrhyncos*
fish crow—*Corvus ossifragus*
blue jay—*Cyanocitta cristata*
northern raven—*Corvus corax*
gray jay—*Perisoreus canadensis*

Chapter 30
Winter Sky

Only imaginary animals here!

Chapter 31
Feathered Denizens of the North

pine siskin—*Carduelis pinus*
rough-legged hawk—*Buteo lagopus*
white-throated sparrow—*Zonotrichia albicollis*
gyrfalcon—*Falco rusticolus*
snowy owl—*Nyctea scandiaca*
common redpoll—*Carduelis flammea*
white-winged crossbill—*Loxia leucoptera*
evening grosbeak—*Coccothraustes vespertinus*
purple sandpiper—*Calidris maritima*
harlequin duck—*Histrionicus histrionicus*

Chapter 32
The Black-capped Chickadee

black-capped chickadee—*Parus atricapillus*
white-breasted nuthatch—*Sitta carolinensis*
red-breasted nuthatch—*Sitta canadensis*
tufted titmouse—*Parus bicolor*
ruby-crowned kinglet—*Regulus calendula*
brown creeper—*Certhia americana*
downy woodpecker—*Picoides pubescens*

APPENDIX FOUR
Natural Areas

Federal Property

Defense Department

- U.S. Navy Property at Calverton (managed by NY State Department of Environmental Conservation)

Fish & Wildlife Service
(516) 286-0485

- Wertheim National Wildlife Refuge — Shirley
- Morton National Wildlife Refuge — Noyack

National Park Service

- Fire Island National Seashore — Islip
- Gateway National Recreation Area
- Floyd Bennett Field
- Jamaica Bay Refuge

New York State Property

Office of Parks, Recreation and Historic Preservation
(516) 669-1000

- Valley Stream State Park — Valley Stream
- Hempstead Lake State Park — Lakeview
- Connetquot River State Park Preserve — Oakdale
- Caumsett State Park — Lloyd Harbor
- Caleb Smith State Park Preserve — Smithtown
- Hither Hills State Park — East Hampton
- Orient Point State Park — Orient
- Brookhaven State Park — Ridge
- Montauk State Park — Montauk
- Planting Fields Arboretum — Upper Brookville
- Jones Beach State Park — Wantagh

- Robert Moses State Park — Islip
- Hecksher State Park — East Islip

Department of Environmental Conservation (516) 444-0270

- Rocky Point Management Area — Rocky Point
- David Sarnoff Preserve — Riverhead
- Edgewood Oak Brush Plains Preserve — Brentwood/Deer Park
- Quogue Wildlife Refuge — Quogue
- Flax Pond Preserve — Old Field

New York City Property

Parks Department

- Forest Park — Brooklyn Manor
- Central Park — Manhattan
- Cunningham Park — Fresh Meadows
- Alley Pond Park — Queens
- Prospect Park —Brooklyn

Nassau County Property

Parks Department
(516) 785-2802

- Cow Meadow Park — Freeport
- Tackapausha Preserve — Seaford
- Massapequa Preserve — Massapequa

Nassau Community College

- Hempstead Plains Preserve — Uniondale (managed by the LI Chapter of The Nature Conservancy, 516-367-3225)

Suffolk County Property

Parks Department
(516) 854-4949

- Montauk County Park — Montauk
- Smith Point County Park — Shirley
- Southaven County Park — Shirley
- West Hills County Park — Huntington
- Blydenburgh County Park — Smithtown
- San Soucci County Park — Sayville

- Sears-Bellows County Park — Hampton Bays
- Cedar Point County Park — East Hampton
- Cedar Beach County Park — Southold
- Hubbard County Park — Flanders
- Indian Island County Park — Riverhead
- Cranberry Bog County Nature Preserve — Riverside
- Shinnecock East & West County Parks — Southampton
- Terrell's River County Park — East Moriches
- Cathedral Pines County Park — Middle Island
- Prosser's Cathedral Pines County Park — Middle Island
- Northwest Harbor County Park — East Hampton
- South Setauket County Conservation Area — South Setauket
- Owl Pond/Birch Creek County Park — Flanders
- Maple Swamp County Park — Flanders
- Goldsmith's Inlet County Park — Peconic
- Robert C. Murphy County Park — Ridge/Manorville
- Lake Ronkonkoma County Park — Ronkonkoma
- Orient Point County Park — Orient

Department of Public Works

- Suffolk County Airport — Westhampton

Town of Babylon Property

Parks Department
(516) 893-2100

- Cedar Beach Park — Babylon
- Overlook Beach Park — Babylon

Town of Brookhaven Property

Parks Department
(516) 451-6100

- West Meadow Beach Park — Old Field

Town of Smithtown Property

(516) 269-1122

Parks Department

- Bill Richards Park — Hauppauge
- Hoyt Farm Park Preserve — Commack

Privately Owned Properties

The Nature Conservancy (516) 367-3225

- Mashomack Preserve — Shelter Island (516) 749-1001
- David Weld Preserve — Nissequogue
- Butler-Huntington Preserve — Nissequogue/St. James
- St John's Pond Preserve — Cold Spring Harbor

North Shore Wildlife Sanctuaries (516) 671-0283

- Shu Swamp — Mill Neck
- Coffin Woods — Matinecock

Index

While growing up in Smithtown, **John Turner** developed his love for nature by exploring the marshes, fields and woodlands along the Nissequogue River. These investigations inspired his strong commitment to conservation issues. He is a co-founder, past-president and current board member of the Long Island Pine Barrens Society and is a former board member of The Long Island Chapter of the Nature Conservancy and the Open Space Council. He has also served on several statewide committees dealing with environmental policy, including the Return-a-Gift-to-Wildlife and Freshwater Wetlands Advisory Committees.

A writer and educator, Turner teaches a series of four courses on environmental management at the Southampton Campus of Long Island University. His many articles on environmental issues have appeared in *Defenders*, *The Conservationist* and *Birder's World*.

John now lives in Massapequa Park with his wife, Georgia, and his two-year-old son, Travis. Following in his father's footsteps, Travis hones his naturalist skills by playing with the family's four dogs and by observing the reaction of the cat when its tail is pulled.